WHY ARE YOU SO FAT?

WHY ARE YOU SO FAT?

The **talkSPORT** Book of
Cricket's Best Ever Sledges

Gershon Portnoi

SIMON &
SCHUSTER

London · New York · Sydney · Toronto

A CBS COMPANY

First published in Great Britain
by Simon & Schuster UK Ltd, 2010
A CBS Company

    5 7 9 10 8 6

Simon & Schuster UK Ltd
1st Floor
222 Gray's Inn Road
London
WC1X 8HB

www.simonandschuster.co.uk

Simon & Schuster Australia
Sydney

A CIP catalogue for this book is available
from the British Library.

ISBN: 978-0-85720-092-1

Typeset and designed by
Craig Stevens and Julian Flanders

All images copyright © Getty Images

Printed and bound in Italy
by L.E.G.O. S.p.A.

Contents

ACKNOWLEDGEMENTS

A huge thank you to everybody who contributed to the book, including (in no particular order): Eddo Brandes, Paul Nixon, Ronnie Irani, Darren Gough, Jack Bannister, Simon Hughes, Chris Cowdrey, Geoffrey Boycott, David Lloyd, Tony Cottey, Rob Badman, Tom Simpson and Richard Ballinger.

Another big thank you to the following people (in no particular order): Daniel Nice, Adam Matthews, Ian Marshall, Jonathan Conway, Gene Portnoi, Dave Lipscomb, Lady Beryl Steinberg, Mich Preston, Stephen Farmer, Adam Bullock and Scott Taunton.

And finally, the people who matter the most. Thanks for your love and support: Victoria and Jake.

▦ INTRODUCTION

A common mantra among sportsmen is 'what goes on in the changing room, stays in the changing room'. This is not a reference to any illicit goings-on, but more a code of honour that meltdowns, tantrums and general behind-the-scenes mayhem are not for public consumption.

Many cricketers have long maintained the motto that 'what goes on on the pitch, stays on the pitch'. This was especially true for cricket's unique form of banter, better known as sledging. Humorous exchanges between bowlers and batsmen have been going on for as long as the game, but these usually remained confidential. Until now...

Thanks to a combination of TV stump microphones, more openness and honesty from professional cricketers and the internet, there has never been a greater appetite for amusing anecdotes from out in the middle. And there can't be any other sports that have such a traditional and distinctive dialogue between opposition players that's become part of the game. Boxers do their talking (in the ring) with their fists, footballers with their feet and golfers with their clubs. None of them stops for a mid-game chat.

So, in the spirit of capturing the public mood, tickling the world's funny bones and swelling my bank account (failed with the last one, hopefully succeeded with the first two), I decided it was high time a comprehensive catalogue of cricket's wittiest, cleverest and rudest sledges was published.

You may notice a high proportion of the banter in this book emerges from the mouths of Australians. This is no coincidence. The Aussies invented sledging and, unlike the English with football, continue to lead the way in their specialised field with aplomb. Indeed, were it not for men like Merv Hughes, Ian Healy and Steve Waugh, it's possible you wouldn't be holding this book in your hands. With an Ashes series coming up later this year (at the time of writing), many of the stories here will whet the appetite.

During my time compiling the book, many friends and colleagues asked me what was my favourite sledge. As you'll discover, there are hundreds in here and, sadly, hundreds more that had to be left out (always leave them wanting more...), so it was a question I always found tough to answer. The truth is, it's impossible to have a favourite. The talkSPORT Top 10 Sledges at the back of the book should go a long way to revealing what most people hold to be the finest examples of this unusual art form.

There are still those who consider sledging vulgar and unnecessary – in fact, Geoffrey Boycott argues the case in these very pages. But, as Simon Hughes also says in this book, 'I think [sledging] is actually important, because you want to see if there's emotion in the game. Competitive sport is compelling to watch because emotions become involved. I think a few words here and there can be entertaining, funny and interesting.'

Amen to that.

Gershon Portnoi
London, July 2010

CHAPTER ONE

SERIAL SLEDGERS

There are sledgers and then there are sledgers. In this chapter, we examine some of the finest exponents of this cricketing art form. These are the players who never let an opportunity to get under an opponent's skin slip by and usually managed to do it with plenty of humour too. **If sledging were a crime, the players featured in this chapter would be doing life sentences…**

▦ MERV HUGHES

☙ Tickling the Ivory

Merv Hughes could have invented sledging – if he'd been born a century earlier. As it was, the Australian fast bowler never missed an opportunity to make up for lost time, playing the game with as much enthusiasm and passion as anyone ever has or will. As famous for his walrus-style bushy moustache as his cricket, Hughes talked a good game – and often backed it up, as 212 wickets in 53 Test matches proves. Hughes saved his best quips for Australia's oldest enemy, England, and was involved in more Ashes confrontations than most.

The worst thing a batsman could do to Hughes – other than clubbing him to the nearest available boundary – was to appear rattled from the bowler's onslaught. In one Ashes Test match, England opening batsman and captain Graham Gooch was finding the going tough, having played and missed at several Hughes deliveries.

The larger-than-life Australian looked far from amused at his misfortune in coming so close to dismissing Gooch. His moustache bristled as he gave Gooch his trademark stare before snarling at the Englishman: 'I'll get you a piano instead – see if you can play that!'

☙ Taking on the Wind-ies

When it comes to verbal sparring out in the middle of an oval, not many people managed to get the better of the great West Indian batsman Viv Richards. So, when the Antiguan and Hughes collided on the pitch, the outcome was always going to be spectacular – or, as in the following case, plain daft.

Richards was a batsman who was never afraid to play his shots and, towards the end of his career, in one particularly memorable over he managed to cart Hughes to the boundary on four consecutive occasions.

The Aussie was the kind of bowler who would produce and hold his famous eyeballing for any batsman who had the temerity to dispatch one of his deliveries to the ropes. So, after four straight boundaries, he was pretty much apoplectic with rage. Hughes walked halfway down the pitch towards the ice-cool West Indian and, just when an ugly confrontation seemed inevitable, he broke wind loudly and said: 'Let's see you hit that to the boundary!'

Taking the Hick

Although he would never admit it, Hughes probably saved his best material for the Ashes – for any self-respecting Aussie cricketer, playing against England is the ultimate encounter where you are required to be on top form with bat, ball and mouth.

Hughes particularly enjoyed winding up England's highly rated batsman Graeme Hick. The Zimbabwe-born cricketer had waited several years to qualify to play for England, but struggled to make an impact at Test level – a fact that was not lost on Hughes.

Merv Hughes has a quiet word with Graeme Hick, after dismissing him in the 1993 Old Trafford Test. The man with the biggest 'tache in cricket was one of the all-time great sledgers.

On one of the first occasions the pair met out in the middle, Hick was enduring a torrid time, failing to make contact with the ball. The Aussie taunted him by saying: 'Mate, if you turn the bat over, you'll see the instructions on the back!'

Another time, Hughes posed Hick the question: 'Does your husband play cricket as well?'

Even legendary English umpire Dickie Bird was rumoured to have stepped in on Hick's behalf when he asked the Australian why he kept yelling at the batsman, to which Hughes responded: 'Dickie, he offended me in a former life.'

Smith on a Pair

As amazing as it may seem, even one of the sport's greatest-ever sledgers could be trumped occasionally. Hughes was certainly never afraid to laugh at himself – he once described the greatest benefit of his magnificently thick and hairy moustache as 'being able to continue to eat breakfast for three hours after the meal' – and he probably would've been guffawing on the inside when England batsman Robin Smith outwitted him at Lord's in 1989.

The old enemy were well on their way to falling 2-0 behind in the six-match series, but that didn't stop Hughes from attempting to put the boot in when Smith came to the crease. After the England number six had played and missed at a beauty from Hughes, the Aussie further tormented his opponent by remarking: 'You can't fucking bat!'

Smith was a gutsy batsman and, shortly after, he smacked Hughes to the boundary, looked up at his adversary and uttered the immortal words: 'Hey Merv! We make a fine pair. I can't fucking bat and you can't fucking bowl!'

For once, the Australian was speechless.

▦ FRED TRUEMAN

↘ Worst Slip

'Fiery Fred' was everything you would expect from an intensely passionate Yorkshire pace bowler. Loud, proud and often extremely amusing to boot, Trueman was one of those once-in-a-generation sportsmen who have something magical about them and never fail to deliver. He had bark and bite. This was equally true when it came to his sledging prowess – he never missed a trick, even when it came to his own team-mates.

Once, during an England v West Indies Test match, Trueman induced an edge from a batsman that travelled towards Raman Subba Row, fielding in the slips. He failed to snare the chance and compounded the close call by allowing the ball to squeeze through his legs and continue merrily on its way to the boundary. Fiery Fred managed to contain himself and simply returned to his mark to bowl the next ball.

At the end of the over, a red-faced Subba Row walked awkwardly towards Trueman: 'Sorry about the catch,' he said.

'What about the bloody four runs?' fumed Trueman.

'Sorry, I should've kept my legs together,' he said, before Trueman looked him in the eye and replied: 'So should your mother!'

↘ Gate Expectations

Many stories are told about Trueman, as the man had achieved legendary status way before the time when that word has become used to describe ordinary sporting folk. The man who once jokingly described himself as 'the greatest bloody fast bowler that ever drew breath' is best summed up by the following anecdotal vignette which demonstrates the wit, arrogance and sheer bloody-mindedness of Trueman.

After the fall of a wicket, an Australian batsman was making his way down the famous Lord's pavilion steps as the next man in. He entered the field of play and just as he was about to turn to shut the gate, Trueman, who was fielding close by, chirped up: 'Don't bother shutting it. You'll be back soon.'

Student Hardship

On equal grounding with the gate quip was Trueman's razor-sharp wit at the expense of a departing Cambridge University batsman. The batsman had been dismissed by the great England bowler and wanted to show his respect and admiration for the Yorkshireman. As he walked back past Trueman on his way back to the pavilion, the student congratulated him, saying: 'That was a very good ball, Mr Trueman.'

Quick as a flash, Trueman responded: 'Aye, lad. Wasted on thee.'

Another university batsman was once on the receiving end when he spent an inordinately long period of time attending to the wicket with his bat before taking strike to face his first ball.

After all the gardening, Trueman, most probably wound up by the undergraduate's irritating wicket-patting, duly dismissed the batsman for a golden duck and then exclaimed: 'Bad luck, sir. You were just getting settled in.'

Settling a Score

The ability to be able to think on his feet enhanced Trueman's legendary status. During a tour of Australia, where Trueman relished locking horns with the locals, the England team were taken on a tour of the outback and Fiery Fred got chatting to a farmer, telling him that his father owned a farm back in Yorkshire.

'How big is your father's farm?' asked the Aussie.

'About twenty acres,' said Trueman. 'Why, how big is yours?'

The Australian replied: 'Well, I'll put it like this: it takes three days to drive a car round it.'

Trueman looked pensive and replied: 'Aye. I used to have a car like that.'

DENNIS LILLEE

If at First You Don't Succeed

Lillee was another moustachioed Australian, albeit with a vastly inferior upper lip growth to the incomparable Merv Hughes, who refused to play quietly. The paceman took no prisoners on or off the pitch and his intensity is best illustrated by his tempestuous relationship with his own captain Kim Hughes.

Unfortunately, Hughes was not on the best of terms with several senior Aussie players and, coupled with the team going through a poor run of form, there was tension in the dressing room. Apart from having verbal spats with his skipper on the pitch (as he once did during a World Series one-day match against New Zealand), Lillee also used to aim bouncers at Hughes during net sessions.

Once, Hughes almost managed to put his head in the way of one of Lillee's howitzers and appeared a little rattled so the bowler asked: 'Did I get you?'

'No, I'm all right,' replied Hughes.

'Then I'll get you next time, you bastard!' said a disappointed Lillee.

Heads You Win

If Lillee was combative with his own team-mates, then he went straight to DEFCON 1 for Ashes Test matches. As far as Lillee was concerned, the English were there to be mocked and roughed up and he particularly enjoyed locking horns with livewire batsman Derek Randall.

Perhaps unfairly, Randall was better known for his extraordinarily athletic fielding than his batting – he was way ahead of his time – but he was more than capable of holding his own as an accomplished middle-order batsman.

Lillee and Randall were involved in several tête-à-tête moments in the Centenary Test in 1977, when England were chasing an extremely unlikely 463 to win and the Englishman struck a Test best 174 to steer his side ever so close. But not close enough.

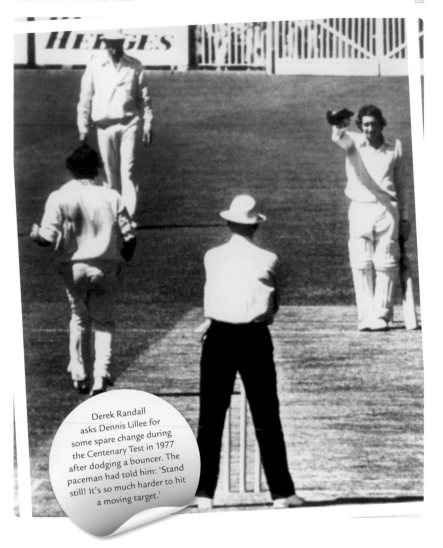

Derek Randall asks Dennis Lillee for some spare change during the Centenary Test in 1977 after dodging a bouncer. The paceman had told him: 'Stand still! It's so much harder to hit a moving target.'

During this innings, after dodging one of many Lillee bouncers, Randall actually doffed his cap to the Australian in acknowledgement at the quality of the delivery. He also received a blow to the head from another Lillee delivery, which he countered by immediately informing the bowler: 'It's no good hitting me there, mate. There's nothing to damage.'

⚑ Batting Lessons

Lillee and Randall were soon at it again, with the Australian coming out on top on points – having failed to knock the Englishman's head clean off.

During this exchange, Lillee was enjoying a period of domination, with Randall failing to make contact with anything the Aussie sent down, despite his best efforts.

After watching Randall take several more air shots, Lillee marched down the wicket towards the hapless batsman and said: 'You just hold the bat out and I'll try to hit it.'

⚑ The End

Like many bowlers at all levels of the game, Lillee had a number of stock sledges that he would employ from time to time if he thought the batsman hadn't heard them before. These weren't necessarily his own gems, but the kind of cricketing banter that has been passed down through generations and is therefore difficult to attribute to any particular player.

He was never short of a line for the press either, once famously describing Geoffrey Boycott as 'The only fellow I've met who fell in love with himself at a young age and has remained faithful ever since.'

One of Lillee's favourites was to inform a struggling batsman his own theory about why he was finding the going so tough: 'I know why you're batting so badly,' he would tell the batsman. 'You've got some shit at the end of your bat.'

At this point, his clueless opponent would lift his bat up and inspect the bottom of it only to find a perfectly clean and unblemished surface. At the same time as the batsman began to realise he was being duped, Lillee would pipe up: 'Wrong end, mate.'

▦ STEVE WAUGH

◥ Older and Wiser

Like many of his predecessors, Australian captain Steve Waugh was a sledger par excellence. He led by example in one of the most awesome and destructive Test teams the sport has ever seen that featured other chirpy players, including Shane Warne and Glenn McGrath.

Playing in his last-ever Test match for his country, Waugh faced a tough situation on the final day at Sydney as he was trying to save the game with India pressing for a series-clinching victory.

Teenage wicketkeeper Parthiv Patel was behind the stumps and he naively thought he could try to distract Waugh from the job in hand. The 18-year-old said: 'Come on Steve. Just one more of your famous slog-sweeps before you finish!'

Waugh turned to his adversary, who was young enough to be his son, and replied: 'Show me some respect. You were still in your diapers when I made my debut.'

And with that, Waugh went on to make a typically defiant 80 to save the match and the series.

Steve Waugh does as he's told by Parthiv Patel during his final, defiant innings for Australia in January 2004. There's no point in trying to sledge a master of the art.

Unfriendly Welcome

Away from Australia, Waugh also spent time playing English county cricket for Kent. Naturally, as an Australian in England, he received his fair share of stick but dished out plenty of his own too.

Once, during an away match at Headingley against Yorkshire, home bowler Steve Kirby took exception to Waugh's very presence at the crease during one over. 'We don't want you here,' roared Kirby. 'Get out of my ground!'

'No, I won't,' replied the Australian. 'This is my favourite pitch. And who are you, the fucking mayor?'

Side Splitting

Waugh's spat with Kirby continued throughout that match with more hilarious consequences. Kirby delighted in mocking Waugh any time he had even the slightest margin of success by beating the bat: 'Australian captain?' he'd ask, as if to suggest he was nowhere near good enough with shots like that.

When Waugh was at the non-striker's end, Kirby decided to change his line of approach and loudly informed the umpire that he was going around the wicket. But the Australian stayed where he was, standing defiantly in the way of the bowler without saying a word.

Unaware that Waugh had not moved to the other side of the stumps, Kirby began his run-up only to stop dead in his tracks when he saw Waugh blocking his path: 'Hey, you! What are you doing there?' he asked angrily.

'I just want to see if you bowl the same sort of shit from this side as you've been bowling from the other side,' replied Waugh as the Yorkshire fielders fell about in hysterics.

▦ SHANE WARNE

◥ Mind Over Matter

The most famous bowler in the history of the game was also well known for his perpetual digs, gripes and swipes at many of the batsmen he exerted such a hold on during his unparalleled career. In fact, it could be argued that part of Warne's success was the psychological grip he could place on a batsman whom he had previously traumatised. Coupled with his extraordinary talent, sometimes Warne only had to make a comment to place doubt in an opponent's mind and the job was as good as done.

One of his staple lines to undermine any opponent who had dared to take a run off his bowling would be to bark at them as they crossed the wicket: 'Where are you going mate, on your holidays?'

Warne had a particularly 'special' relationship with South African batsman Daryll Cullinan, a brilliant player who became something of a 'rabbit' for Warne during the pair's battles. Warne did his homework, and before one Test match he read how the South African had spent time seeing a psychologist to overcome some mental barriers on the pitch. There are many players who would've waded straight in with brash and thoughtless sledges upon discovering this information, but Warne was cleverer than that.

When Cullinan walked to the wicket, the leg spinner said nothing. He watched as the South African strolled around the pitch, did a spot of gardening and prepared himself for the challenge ahead before simply asking him: 'What colour was the couch?'

◥ A Matter of Honours

Sometimes, Warne could be far more aggressive and direct towards an opponent as was the case in the 2006-07 Ashes Test series in Australia. This was a series which the Aussies were even more desperate to win than usual after surrendering the urn to the English in 2005 for the first time in two decades – and that might help explain why Warne decided to call England batsman Ian Bell 'The Sherminator' all series, in reference to a character from the film *American Pie* whom he thought Bell resembled.

Durham grit meets Aussie wit – it's another sledging hit!

England's 2005 celebrations had been suitably over the top, with an open-top bus tour of central London followed by the entire Ashes squad receiving MBEs from the Queen. Even Paul Collingwood, who only played in the deciding rubber at The Oval and contributed seven runs in the first innings and ten in the second, was awarded a gong.

Like an old elephant, Warne had not forgotten this and, as the Aussies were well on their way to rubbing England's noses in it with a series whitewash to reclaim the Ashes, he waited until the final Test to have his say. And as England were sliding to another defeat, Warne was batting and Collingwood attempted to sledge him from point, giving the Aussie the perfect opportunity: 'You got an MBE, right? For scoring seven at The Oval? That's embarrassing!'

■ Defence is the Best Form of Attack

Warne's knack of unnerving opponents was never more evident than when he encouraged players to take him on – with inevitable consequences. During a match in India, the home side were batting and Sourav Ganguly was in the middle alongside the great Sachin

Tendulkar. Warne was bowling to Ganguly, who had allowed a couple of fairly loose deliveries to go by without attempting a shot. The Aussie strode down the wicket and asked Ganguly: 'What are you doing?'

The nonplussed batsman said nothing, and Warne continued: 'Look, all the fans here have bought tickets to see this guy [pointing to Tendulkar] play his shots, not to watch you defending.'

The comment clearly riled Ganguly as, shortly after, he charged down the wicket to Warne attempting a big hit, completely misread the flight of the ball and was duly stumped.

⠿ IAN HEALY

⠃ Nasser by a Nose

Aside from possibly Paul Nixon, to whom we will come in good time, Ian Healy was possibly the noisiest man to keep wicket in the modern era. The Australian was never short of something to say, from his famed 'Bowling, Warnie' to any number of subtle digs and mind games aimed at spoiling a batsman's concentration. And his questionable tactics often paid off, as was the case when he helped dismiss Nasser Hussain in an Ashes Test.

Captain Steve Waugh was rearranging his field and decided to place Ricky Ponting at silly point to put Hussain off. 'I want you right under his nose,' Waugh told his fielder, only for Healy to chip in: 'That would be anywhere inside a three-mile radius!'

The England skipper saw the funny side, although probably a little too much as he burst into fits of laughter and was dismissed three balls later.

⠃ Shiver me Timbers

Healy was also involved in several hilarious exchanges with Arjuna Ranatunga, the portly Sri Lanka skipper and batting great. Neither man would ever be described as a shrinking violet, and so it proved whenever the pair clashed out in the middle.

In one match, the Aussies were attempting to rough up Ranatunga with some aggressive bowling so Healy inquired if the tactics had made the Sri Lankan nervous: 'Got your legs shivering?' inquired the wicketkeeper.

Ian Healy got right up Nasser Hussain's nose with his sledging.

But he was well and truly stumped when Ranatunga replied: 'Yes, I'm tired after sleeping with your wife!' It was one of the rare occasions that Healy was lost for words.

Butchering England

The 1998-99 Ashes series in Australia saw England outplayed for four out of the five Tests, and Healy revelled in the old enemy's misery. After three matches in which England's opening partnership had failed to fire, Mark Butcher moved down to bat at number three to make way for Alec Stewart to open with Mike Atherton.

Unfortunately, an early wicket in the first innings meant Butcher was taking his guard from the umpire inside the first over and the same thing happened in England's second innings, albeit an over later. Healy couldn't help himself the second time around and, as Butcher arrived at the crease, he piped up: 'Not much different at number three, is it Butch?'

CHRIS COWDREY

Mike Gatting was an easy target throughout his career due to the bulk he tended to carry around with him. The Middlesex and England batsman was a class act on the pitch, but that didn't stop opponents making merry at his expense – in fact, his own team-mates were probably worst of all, as Chris Cowdrey recalls:

' David Gower, the England captain, was giving me my first-ever bowl during a Test match against India in Calcutta. We were at the start of my run-up having a chat about what field we should have.

India had already made a massive score so, in typical Gower fashion, he was saying: **"Oh, we'd better have someone out there, a couple out there and someone out there."**

Then he said: **"You've got one slip in. It's Gatting at slip. Do you want him a bit wider?"** So I replied: **"If he was any wider, he'd burst!"** and he absolutely collapsed in laughter.

It took about 20 minutes for it to go all around the field, everybody was laughing. The person who hadn't heard it was Mike Gatting, who was a very great friend of mine, and eventually it got to him and, of course, he laughed. It was great fun.

That one is so unusual as it was a sledge of my own team-mate and most of a team's sledging goes against the opposition. That's my favourite as I think I should stay famous for sledging my own team-mate.'

In fact, Cowdrey wasn't the only one to take advantage of Fat Gatt, as he was known. Aside from his infamous spat with Pakistani umpire Shakoor Rana, Gatting was most famous for being the victim of the famous Shane Warne dismissal that became known as the 'Ball of the Century' during the Old Trafford Ashes Test in 1993.

Yet even being the unfortunate recipient of a ball that turned such a huge distance did not mean Gatting was to escape the jibes of his own colleagues. When asked about the wicket, Graham Gooch once commented: 'If it had been a cheese roll, it would never have got past him.'

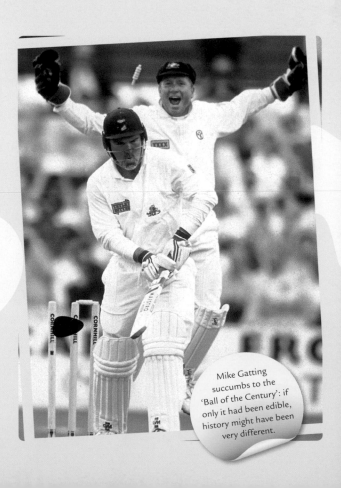

Mike Gatting succumbs to the 'Ball of the Century': if only it had been edible, history might have been very different.

CHAPTER TWO

WEIGHTY ISSUES

Despite the physical excellence that is demanded from the increasingly more professional sport of cricket, there have been many players over the years who have taken the lunch and tea breaks far too literally for their own good. This chapter is dedicated to them. The sitting ducks of the sledging world. The players who could never be described as athletes, but who still made a decent living out of the game. Just like picking on the overweight kid at school, so cricketers will always round (no pun intended) on the player who looks out of shape. **Fat cricket blokes: this one's for you.**

▥ COOKIE MONSTER

To most cricket fans 26 August 1996 is not a memorable date. The first match of the Singer World Series, a one-day competition between India, Sri Lanka, Australia and Zimbabwe, was never going to be the talk of the cricketing world, but for one man – and for sledging fans across the globe – everything was about to change.

Even the context in which it happened was as insignificant as any you could find in cricket. With Zimbabwe staring down the barrel of a heavy defeat and those gathered in Colombo's R.Premadasa Stadium probably completely disinterested, bulky last man Eddo Brandes strolled to the crease, intent on having some fun in a lost cause as the match was over as a contest.

Aussie paceman Glenn McGrath wanted to finish the match in a hurry and became increasingly frustrated as Brandes, attempting a big heave-ho, swung his bat and missed on several occasions. McGrath, clearly anxious to put his feet up for the day, was aggravated enough to look Brandes up and down and go for the jugular: 'Why are you so fat?' he enquired.

Quick-as-a-flash, the portly Zimbabwean retorted: 'Because every time I make love to your wife, she gives me a biscuit!'

For Brandes, life would never be the same again although he remains hazy on the events of that day and slightly embarrassed: 'I can't say I really remember that much about it. I didn't think much of it at the time. These things happen, you don't plan them. I said something along those lines, but the words get twisted over time. Sometimes I'd also like to be remembered for playing cricket. It's frustrating to be remembered for the wrong things.'

It's fair to say that millions of people around the world believe he's remembered for the right thing.

▥ CHOCA-BLOCKER

Sri Lanka's Arjuna Ranatunga was a magnificent cricketer but always struggled with his weight, and it was no surprise that he became the butt of many sledging jokes throughout his career. Perhaps the best and most famous moment came during a match against Australia in which Ian Healy was keeping wicket.

The Australian was hardly the most subtle of sledgers at the best of times and Ranatunga's large presence at the crease was an open goal waiting to be tapped in. As the Aussies began to get frustrated with the Sri Lankan's stubborn resistance at the wicket, Healy suddenly yelled out to his bowler with a revolutionary idea to tempt Ranatunga into playing a false stroke: 'Put a Mars bar on a good length, that should do it!'

 ## PLAY IT AGAIN, IAN

That was clearly a line Healy kept towards the front of his sledging locker, because he was at it again during an Australian tour match against Hansie Cronje's South African Free State side.

Cronje was batting alongside a rather chunky-looking team-mate and when the unfortunately rotund player came on strike, Healy immediately advised Shane Warne to 'Bowl a Mars bar halfway down. We'll get him stumped!'

On this occasion though, the batsman joined in with the japes and, seeing an oversized David Boon fielding close by, retorted: 'No, Boonie fielding at short leg will be onto it before I can move.'

 ## NO RUNNER-TUNGA

Healy clearly had a thing for the larger man. This time, back in January 1996, Ranatunga was again the victim during the second match of the World Series final. Australia had scored 273 from their 50 overs in the match, only for a deluge of rain to curtail the start of Sri Lanka's reply. Eventually, the visitors were set a target of 168 from 25 overs in extremely humid conditions at the Sydney Cricket Ground.

Ranatunga was attempting to guide his side to a series-levelling victory, but was certainly feeling the effect of the heavy atmosphere and

WHY ARE YOU SO FAT?

began to perspire at an extraordinary rate. With exhaustion setting in, the Sri Lankan claimed he had sprained an ankle and therefore required a runner, much to the consternation of the wicketkeeper, who exclaimed: 'You don't get a runner for being an overweight, unfit, fat c***!'

Incredibly, umpire Steve Randell seemed to agree with Healy – although probably not by using the same words – and turned down Ranatunga's request, although it was granted the following over when Sanath Jayasuriya came out to run for his captain.

But it was all to no avail as the 'overweight, unfit, er, one' was out for 41 and Sri Lanka eventually fell short of their target by nine runs.

▦ HUNGRY FOR SUCCESS

The ongoing feud between Daryll Cullinan and Shane Warne has already been touched upon, but it wasn't often that the South African came out on top in exchanges between the pair. More often than not, Warne would take Cullinan's wicket and, whatever pleasantries had been exchanged between the pair, the Australian would allow his bowling to have the final say.

However, Warne's one weakness throughout his career was probably his weight, which swung more than a seam-tampered cricket ball. Once, he stormed out of the unveiling of his waxwork double when a reporter asked him if he preferred the shape of the model to his own. It's not unreasonable to deduce he was touchy about his size.

Even his own team-mates ribbed him about it, as Ian Healy once declared: 'Shane Warne's idea of a balanced diet is a cheeseburger in each hand.'

Cue the 1999 World Cup Super Six clash between Australia and South Africa at Headingley, and Cullinan coming out to the middle at the fall of the first wicket. Before the game, Warne had been taunting Cullinan, claiming he could get him out with an orange, and the Aussie greeted his opponent warmly: 'I've been waiting two years for another chance to humiliate you.'

The South African looked Warne up and down before replying: 'Looks like you spent it eating.'

He went on to make exactly 50 from 60 balls, but guess who managed to end his spell at the crease? That chubby leg spinner, of course.

FEELING SHEEPISH

Pre-match sledging is rare, but can be as spectacular as two boxers having a war of words in the build-up to a big fight. Our fat friends Ranatunga and Warne were at the centre of the action again as the Australians touched down in Sri Lanka at the beginning of the 2004 Test series. By this time, Ranatunga had actually retired but was still actively involved in his nation's cricket set-up.

The series coincided with Warne's return to international cricket after a 12-month suspension for taking a banned diuretic. The Aussie has gone on record more than once for his dislike of Ranatunga, saying: 'Frankly, Sri Lanka – and the game overall – would be better off without him [Ranatunga]. I don't like him and I'm not in a club of one.'

Arjuna Ranatunga (left), a few years after his retirement, discusses his options for lunch.

Warne was clearly chomping at the bit at the prospect of taking the field again and landed the first blow when he told Melbourne's *Daily Mirror*: 'He's [Ranatunga] probably slotting himself around at one hundred and fifty kilos at the moment. Swallowed a sheep or something.'

But Ranatunga, in a clear reference to Warne's ban, quickly hit back, telling the press: 'It is better to swallow a sheep or a goat than swallow what he has been swallowing.'

RESTRICTED VIEW

Sledging legend Dennis Lillee was still going strong in 1994 at the ripe old age of 45, although by then he had retired from all forms of first-class cricket. But he was there to welcome the English tourists for the impending Ashes series in the first warm-up match of the tour, a one-day game in Perth. Lillee was part of an Australian Cricket Board Chairman's XI that also featured other former greats including Jeff Thomson, Rod Marsh and Greg Chappell.

A game like that was always going to be played in good spirits and Lillee led by example. When the notoriously 'stocky' Mike Gatting was taking strike against Lillee, the Australian began his run-up to the stumps before stopping and yelling to the England batsman: 'Move out of the way, Gatt. I can't see the stumps!'

BEANS MEANS ZAHEER SHINES

Arguably the most bizarre sledge in cricket history has to be the curious incident at the Trent Bridge Test between England and India in 2007 when not a word was said.

When tailender Zaheer Khan arrived at the crease to take guard in India's first innings, the swing bowler found a jelly bean on the pitch. He promptly moved the sweet off the wicket only to find that more had appeared after the next ball. This led to a furious exchange

between Khan and several England players, with the Indian eventually waving his bat threateningly towards Kevin Pietersen.

It still remains unclear who threw the beans on the pitch and what was their exact purpose, but the most likely explanation is that they were a vague insult at the weight problems with which Khan had been struggling earlier in the year. Either that, or England were just bored as India piled up a lead of close to 300 runs.

The bowler certainly didn't find the prank funny, and England were left rueing the incident when he claimed five wickets the following day to steer India to victory and then declared that he'd been motivated by the jelly bean incident: 'I felt it was insulting. When I go out there on the field, I'm serious. This is Test match cricket we're playing. No one has told me what it means but it gave me motivation. It inspired me to do well.'

Despite the controversy, England took an altogether more light-hearted approach to the stunt, with Paul Collingwood's analysis of the incident causing guffaws up and down the country: 'He wasn't too pleased. I think he prefers the blue ones to the pink ones.'

LADIES NOT GENTLEMEN

And finally, anyone under the misapprehension that weight, size and shape sledging cruelness was confined to men's cricket has clearly never watched a women's game.

If the so-called gentlemanly game has long since become ungentlemanly, then the same can certainly be said for the women's game being unladylike, as bad language is commonplace.

And those girls are arguably worse than the blokes, if reports from a 1990s Ashes series are anything to go by, as an unnamed England player revealed her ordeal at the hands – and mouths – of the Australians while batting: 'The slip fielders kept saying I had a big backside and the wicketkeeper asked me if you had to be ugly to get into the England side.'

And, similar to the men's game, instead of blubbing at the old meanies, the players use the abuse for motivation: 'It was irritating, but it made me more determined to do well,' she continued. 'They were very quiet when I hit a four.'

Women sledging? They'll give them the vote, next...

JACK BANNISTER

When a team fields a batting line-up consisting of a long list of vertically challenged players, they're asking for trouble. And when 6ft 2in England off-spinner John Emburey is bowling, the comedy ingredients are ready to be shaken up and cooked into something special.

Emburey was not necessarily a man known for his sledging on the pitch. A steely-nerved and determined competitor, Emburey plied his trade for Middlesex and it was during a county match against Glamorgan in the early 1990s that the incident occurred that still tickles the ribs of talkSPORT cricket correspondent Jack Bannister.

In the game, the Welsh side featured Hugh Morris, who was 5ft 8in, and Tony Cottey, who came in at 5ft 4in – but they were just the tip of the iceberg. Emburey managed to remove Cottey, and in walked Alistair Dalton, not much taller than the man he replaced.

The spinner quickly took care of Dalton and Stuart Phelps walked to the wicket, himself another couple of inches shorter than Dalton. It wasn't long before the magician had struck with the ball again. But this time Steve Barwick strode out to the middle, all 6ft 2in of him, with long, black hair sticking out of his helmet.

Emburey looked up and, startled, called out to his captain Mike Gatting: **'Fuck me, Gatt. We've had all the dwarves – who's this? Snow White?'**

For Glamorgan batsman Cottey, it wasn't the first – and certainly not the last – time he'd been ridiculed

MY FAVOURITE SLEDGE

about his height. Or lack of it. Once, during a NatWest Trophy one-day match, the Welsh county were playing in front of a boisterous crowd against Nottinghamshire at Trent Bridge. 'I was fielding in front of Castle Corner,' explained Cottey. 'They're all pissed, about two thousand of them, and I got plenty of abuse. We were ten for four when I came in to bat. I put one foot on the ground and the whole stand started singing "Hi Ho!" all the way to the wicket.'

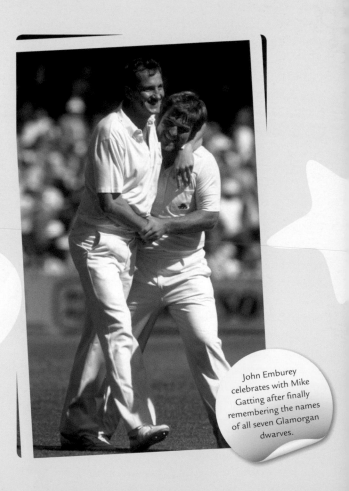

John Emburey celebrates with Mike Gatting after finally remembering the names of all seven Glamorgan dwarves.

CHAPTER THREE

WHEN ALL ELSE FAILS... SWEAR!

In the heat of battle, it's not always that convenient to summon up a witticism of which Oscar Wilde himself would have been proud. Instead, many cricketers resort to what is commonly referred to as 'colourful' language. **This is the section whose anecdotes you won't be reading out in front of your wife, kids or parents. At least not on purpose at any rate. You have been warned...**

BOILING OVER IN THE CARIBBEAN

The most tragically hilarious and vulgar sledge of all took place when Australia were touring the West Indies in 2003. The tourists were on the verge of a whitewash, as the Windies needed to chase a world-record 417 to win the match in front of a noisy Antiguan crowd unwavering in their support for their heroes.

But 22-year-old Ramnaresh Sarwan had other ideas and began compiling a wonderful innings of 105 to spare his side's blushes as they recorded an astonishing win. While he was batting, Glenn McGrath was attempting to move hell and high water to ensure the Australians achieved the victory he believed they merited. But things were not going according to plan and, as the paceman conceded 21 runs in two overs, he boiled over.

His opening gambit to Sarwan was: 'So what does Brian Lara's cock taste like?'

The youngster immediately replied: 'I don't know. Ask your wife.'

And McGrath exploded, storming down the wicket to confront Sarwan: 'You mention my fucking wife again and I'll rip your fucking throat out!'

Sadly, McGrath's late wife Jane was fighting cancer at the time, hence his combative reaction. But Sarwan wasn't to know that and McGrath had patently started the trouble.

Many would call the incident shameful, indeed the Australian Cricket Board was forced to remind Steve Waugh's side about the spirit of cricket. But the truth is that players had been trading insults on a regular basis for

Sarwan and McGrath discuss a potential double date.

years, so the gentlemanly side of the game had long since disappeared. And for that we have to be thankful or there would be no sledging.

 ## AN ILLEGITIMATE TRUTH

During the intense exchanges of the Bodyline Ashes series in 1932-33, a complaint was made by controversial England captain Douglas Jardine to his Australian counterpart, Bill Woodfull. That's the same Woodfull who was struck close to the heart by a Harold Larwood delivery – who was bowling under Jardine's specific instructions.

Jardine's complaint was that one of Woodfull's charges had called him a bastard.

Together, the captains marched into the Aussies' dressing room and, in front of his entire team, the Australian skipper pointed to the Englishman and uttered the immortal line: 'Which one of you bastards called this bastard a bastard?'

 ## PARORE DECLARES WAUGH

As much as Australia dislike the 'Poms', they're none too keen on their Kiwi neighbours either. Recent Australia v New Zealand clashes have been contested with as much intensity as some Ashes showdowns with rivalries developing between players that lasted through different series. And there was certainly no love lost between Mark Waugh and New Zealand's wicketkeeper/batsman Adam Parore during a 1990s tour of the islands.

Parore came to the wicket, had a swish at his first ball but wasn't even close to making contact and Waugh, fielding at second slip, sprung into action. 'Oh, I remember you from a couple of years ago in Australia,' said Waugh. 'You were shit then and you're fucking useless now.'

Parore turned around to face Waugh and replied: 'Yeah, that's me and when I was there you were going out with that old ugly slut. Now I hear you've married her, you dumb c***.'

Adam Parore and Mark Waugh show their mutual delight at renewing their acquaintance.

▦ CULTURE CLASH

It's not easy to follow a riposte like that, so who better to turn to than one of the greatest merchants of crudities, Merv Hughes? As previously discussed, when he wasn't shooting his mouth off in the direction of the nearest batsman, Hughes would instead resort to his most menacing stare, which he would hold for as long as it took an opponent to look away.

During a tour of the West Indies, Hughes was bowling to Viv Richards at Antigua and employed one of his fiercest stares for one of the world's greatest batsmen. But Richards was not having it. Not one bit. 'This is my island, my culture,' he said. 'In my culture we don't stare. We just go back and bowl.'

Unfortunately for Richards, this was one of those rare occasions where his batting couldn't support his brave words and Hughes soon captured his wicket. As the home favourite departed, Hughes saw him off with this parting shot: 'In my culture we just say fuck off.'

EYEING EACH OTHER UP

A similar clash occurred a few years later between Steve Waugh and Curtly Ambrose, only this time it was the West Indian who was doing the eyeballing. The Aussies were attempting to win in the Caribbean for the first time in a generation and they were ahead going into the third of four Tests at the Queen's Park Oval in Trinidad in April 1995.

But, in a remarkable game where the highest score was 136, things did not pan out for Mark Taylor's team, especially when they found themselves three wickets down with just 14 on the board on the first morning.

That meant Waugh entered the fray and a ferocious duel ensued between him and Ambrose, with the West Indian launching a full-scale assault of leather-bound round missiles at the Australian. The longer Waugh remained at the crease, the longer and more intense Ambrose's angry stares at the batsman became until he cracked.

'What the fuck are you looking at?' Waugh asked.

Not many cricketers decided that it was a wise move to anger 6ft 8in speed merchant Curtly Ambrose when he had a ball in his hand; but then Steve Waugh wasn't like many cricketers.

Ambrose was stunned. That sort of question had not been posed to him that often in his career, and he stepped closer towards Waugh and said firmly: 'Don't cuss me, man.'

As Waugh later admitted in his autobiography, at that moment 'Nothing inventive or witty came to mind, rather another piece of personal abuse,' and he put himself at considerable risk by suggesting to Ambrose: 'Why don't you go and get fucked?'

Before the situation deteriorated into a major incident, Windies captain Richie Richardson dragged his bowler away although he was clearly reluctant not to finish what he had started. For the record, nobody was able to drag Waugh away from the crease in that innings and he was the only batsman in the match to pass 50, but it was in vain as Australia lost. They did, however, win the decider to claim that elusive series win.

▦ GARDENING LEAVE

Richie Benaud has achieved almost deific status in both England and Australia thanks to his work in the commentary box since retiring as a player. So it's hard to imagine he could ever have been involved in the type of skulduggery that not only takes place on these pages, but also in this specific chapter.

Thankfully, he was merely the victim of this particular piece of cricket hooliganism, so Benaud's reputation remains unblemished. In the famous 'Laker Test' at Old Trafford in 1956 (in which English spinner Jim Laker claimed the absurd and mind-boggling match figures of 19 for 90 against Australia), the man to claim the other Australian wicket was Tony Lock. But 'Lockie' must have been frustrated to prise out only one Aussie, as he watched his spin companion decimate the tourists.

Towards the end of the game, Lockie let his irritation become public when bowling to Benaud, who was trying to waste as much time as possible by indulging in long spells of gardening between every delivery.

Benaud's one-man mission to flatten out the pitch was abruptly halted when he played a defensive stroke that rolled into Lock's hands. The bowler then hurled the ball straight to wicketkeeper Godfrey Evans, via the nasal hairs and eyebrows of the Australian, and bellowed: 'Tap that one down, you little bastard!'

KEEPING UP WITH JONES

Dean Jones was known for his confidence, bordering on cockiness, which itself bordered on falling in love with himself. In his defence, he has been credited with almost single-handedly rewriting the manual for one-day cricket, such was the impact his style of play made on the modern game. And, with an average of more than 46 in Tests and a fraction less in limited-overs cricket, it's hard to argue with the theory that if you can walk the walk, you're entitled to talk the talk. But not everybody subscribed to that particular rationale and Jones was forced to put up with plenty of criticism throughout his career.

It's rumoured that during a Sheffield Shield match, a rookie spinner was bowling to Jones and started to lay into the batsman with a few choice remarks.

Unhappy with the chutzpah of the youngster, Jones simply shot back with: 'Don't you know who I am, mate?'

'Yeah,' said the bowler. 'You're the biggest c*** in Australian cricket.'

MANNERS MAKETH MAN... ANGRY

When Graham Gooch strode out to the Edgbaston wicket for his Test debut in 1975, he must have thought he had the world at his feet. Still 21 years old, the fresh-faced Essex batsman was playing in the biggest match of his life, the first Ashes Test of the summer, and seemed to be relishing it.

As he walked past the tourists' captain, Ian Chappell, he courteously bid him: 'Good morning, Ian.'

Graham Gooch tried to give the Aussies a lesson in manners, but they didn't want to listen and dismissed him for a pair on his Test debut.

All was well with the world. Until about two seconds later when Chappell barked at him: 'What's so fucking good about it?'

It must have made an impact on Gooch, as three balls later he was on his way back to the pavilion. And if that sounds like a nightmare debut, it soon worsened as the Essex man bagged a pair with a second-innings duck in a heavy defeat for England. Good morning, indeed.

EVEN BORED-ER

After overseeing two previous defeats to England, Allan Border meant business on the 1989 Ashes tour, but perhaps nobody told England paceman Angus Fraser.

Despite being a 6ft 6in seamer who relished the opportunity to hit line and length on an almost metronomically regular basis, making things as uncomfortable as possible for a batsman, Fraser was one of the game's nice guys.

Perhaps his genteel English nature, which was subsequently heard over the airwaves when he followed his career with a stint as a journalist and broadcaster, was not ideally suited to duels with no-nonsense, in-your-face Australians like Border.

When the pair squared up for the first time, Fraser seemed to be having some success. Buoyed by going narrowly past the edge of Border's bat, the gentle giant of a bowler made a couple of sarcastic digs at the Aussie captain.

But Border was clearly not in the mood. 'I've faced bigger, uglier bowlers than you, mate,' he snapped. 'Now fuck off and bowl the next one.'

Gus Fraser may have had to wait four years, but he still got his revenge over Allan Border in the 1993 Oval Test: who's ugly now?

▦ THIS WAY TO THE PAVILION, SIR

If you've spent a whole session getting spanked all over the park by a batsman, it's bound to be tempting to see him off with a little gusto when you finally get rid of him. Except most people don't. But Darren Gough ain't most people.

England's most charismatic cricketer of his era was toiling under a barrage of boundaries from Sachin Tendulkar and Sourav Ganguly in a limited-overs international in India and becoming increasingly frustrated. The game was pretty much over and India were cantering home, but Gough still had his own personal scores to settle.

Having tempted Ganguly with a slower ball, the ploy worked and the batsman's off stump was uprooted. As Gough directed Ganguly back to the dressing rooms behind him with a flick of his thumb, TV footage also clearly showed him saying: 'Fuck off! Go on, fuck off!'

And it wasn't the only time Gough performed the stunt after a dismissal: 'Sometimes, the adrenaline's buzzing when you get someone out,' he explained. 'I've sent a few off in my career; there's nowt wrong with that. I've also been sent off. If someone's been slogging you all over the place, it's almost like he's won; but if you get them out it makes you feel as though you've won, even if they win the match.'

DARREN GOUGH

Until the introduction of Freddie Flintoff to the international scene in the late 1990s, Darren Gough was probably the closest thing England had to an Ian Botham-type character on and off the pitch. So it's little surprise to find that Goughie has nominated a Beefy sledge as his preferred choice.

' I do like the one with Beefy and Rod Marsh,' Gough explained. 'It's absolute quality. That's the sort of humour I like. I thought it was really good.'

For such an animated, exuberant and colourful personality, there are relatively few recorded Botham sledging stories. No matter though, because Gough's choice stands head and shoulders above almost all others in any case.

In the 1970s and 1980s, the England and Australian cricketers used to have an extremely jovial relationship on and off the pitch, playing hard then often partying hard together after a day's cricket. That meant there was no shortage of banter on the field of play and, if anything, some of the sledging became even funnier the more time the opposing players spent together away from the middle.

Wicketkeeper Rod Marsh was as central to shenanigans on and off the pitch as anyone and, during the first Test of an Ashes series, he welcomed Botham to the wicket by asking: **'So, how's your wife and my kids?'**

That would be good enough on its own, but Botham had the good

Ian Botham poses with his wife and children just before he headed out to Australia in 1986 to help England win the Ashes Down Under for the last time to date.

grace and class to reply with: 'The wife's fine, but the kids are retarded.'

The great man himself was gracious enough to once admit: 'I did enjoy Rod Marsh's quip,' although he was disparaging about the Australians and their sledging abilities in general.

'The Aussies are not particularly smart or clever when it comes to sledging and towards the end of my career they actually started to get a bit nasty rather than funny.'

But Beefy has also admitted he was a great fan of the banter out in the middle, although he used it sparingly: 'I loved sledging – thrived on it. But you only sledge someone you can affect. I'd never sledge Allan Border or Steve Waugh or Viv Richards. I didn't want to wake them up. The soft guys – you nail them. It's the predator instinct. Dog eat dog.'

CHAPTER FOUR

MIND GAMES

If this chapter could have been brought to you in association with Sir Alex Ferguson, it would have been. Unfortunately, Fergie was unavailable for cricket book chapter sponsorships, but the man who has made managerial mind games a modern football phenomenon would be proud of these cricketing equivalents.

These are the sledges that were specifically uttered to cause doubt or a loss of concentration in an opponent's mind. And the hope was that would translate into enough of an advantage to make a difference to the outcome of a match. **The only problem is that sometimes playing mind games can have quite the opposite effect...**

▦ TALKING IN TONGUES

The lengths some teams will go to for a psychological edge is extraordinary – in some cases involving complex kidology. When Glamorgan played the South Africans in a tour match at Pontypridd, Tony Cottey and David Hemp shared a decent stand until they were rudely interrupted by the tourists.

'They started speaking Afrikaans to each other,' explained Cottey. 'They were saying Cottey and Hemp at the end of each sentence and then laughing. It was like mental disintegration – they did it to quite a few of us and it was very uncomfortable. Crofty [Robert Croft] didn't like it.'

But, the Welsh county realised they could repeat the trick themselves, given the unique mother tongue of some of the players. During another tour match, the following year, Cottey and his team-mates hatched a cunning plan: 'Crofty could speak a little bit of pidgin Welsh and I spoke a bit too,' he said.

'We were playing Australia A who had a great side – Elliott, Love, Law, Ponting, Langer, Gilchrist – anyway, we decided that when we were out in the middle we'd only speak Welsh. All the boys that couldn't speak it would have a Welsh phrase and we'd get into them. Even Neil Kendrick, from Bromley in Kent, had a phrase "Hufen ia, Langer", which meant "Ice cream, Langer" – there was no rhyme or reason to it. Kendrick was shouting it and it really did piss Langer off, because Crofty got him out. For one hundred and thirty-six! Anything to get an edge.'

▦ OFF WITH THEIR HEADS!

The much-maligned England 'Bodyline' team who controversially triumphed in Australia in the 1932-33 Ashes series were not just infamous for their practice of intimidatory bowling techniques. No, those boys were just as big on the mental side of the game, even all those years ago.

Before the series had even started, England and Nottinghamshire bowler Bill Voce, the other half of the country's opening attack alongside Harold Larwood, famously told Australian vice-captain Vic Richardson (grandfather of the Chappell brothers) about England's intentions: 'If we don't beat you, we'll knock your bloody heads off!'

Waiting for heads to roll – Bill Voce makes his intentions pretty clear.

Crude statements like that were far ahead of their time and went a long way to giving England a psychological advantage – especially when Larwood & Co backed up the threat on the pitch. The third, and most controversial, Test match at Adelaide, described by *Wisden* as 'probably the most unpleasant Test ever played' was where the real action kicked off, as Larwood felled Australian captain Bill Woodfull with a delivery that struck him on the chest. At that point, England skipper Douglas Jardine piped up with: 'Well bowled, Harold,' which served only to inflame tensions further.

With no protection to players available in those days other than a box, England won the Test (and subsequently the series) as much by scaring the Australians as physically damaging them – Bert Oldfield suffered a fractured skull from another Larwood ball. These were old-fashioned mind games where players practised what they preached.

⠿ TAIL-ENDERS RULE

Fast forward 40 years, and the old enemies were still at it, although Jardine's 'leg theory' had long since been abolished. But players were still getting struck – this time, however, they wore protection.

England's Tony Greig was giving tail-ender Dennis Lillee a thorough going over and managed to hit the Aussie with a short ball. What fielding teams often forget in these situations is that it won't be long before the part-time batsman has the ball in his hand. Completely missing that point, England fielder Keith Fletcher congratulated Greig, saying: 'Well done! Give him another one.'

Lillee composed himself and looked over to Fletcher and warned: 'It'll soon be your turn.'

David Lloyd remembers that the incident proved Lillee wasn't joking: 'When it was Fletcher's turn the following day, Lillee walked him in! He went right across to the gate and walked in with Fletch. And he almost took guard with him in front of the stumps!'

⠿ TUFFERS' TERROR

A similar moment to the Lillee threat occurred between Craig McDermott and Phil Tufnell during an Ashes Test at Perth, renowned as one of the quickest wickets in the world at that time, in February 1991. Tuffers was playing in his first Ashes series and picked up a couple of wickets towards the end of the Australian innings, including the dismissal of McDermott.

For some reason, the number nine was unhappy at being bowled by England's new spinner and, as he departed, turned to Tufnell and menacingly said: 'You've got to bat on this in a minute, Tufnell. Hospital food suit you?'

If ever there was a rabbit of a batsman it was Tufnell, who remarkably came in at number ten, ahead of Devon Malcolm, so McDermott's 'in a minute' was clearly also a dig at the entire England batting line-up. But he must have known something, as he took three wickets in England's dismal 182 all out. Tuffers' team-mates were obviously not keen on hospital grub either.

▦ HEAD TO HEAD

Darren Gough is convinced that mind games play a huge role in cricket and determining the outcome of a series. On his first Ashes tour in 1994-95, the teams were required to have pictures taken together and Gough found himself face to face with Merv Hughes.

'I made a point of trying to be brave and stood up to him and stared him out,' recalled Gough. 'For me, that was a big step and they probably thought "who the fuck's this young whippersnapper squaring up to Merv?" who's a legend in Australia. I never backed down and it helped me.'

Four years later, at the start of another tour, England were playing Western Australia at Perth in a warm-up match and Gough was determined to score some psychological points against batsman Justin Langer, who would be playing for the Aussies in the first Test.

'I tried to be aggressive but he came back with "You're in my town now", which I thought was quite humorous,' said Gough. 'I said something about his missus, I think, just jokingly of course. He tried to slog me all over the place so he bit and I got him out. It worked, didn't it?'

It worked even better when Gough dismissed Langer cheaply at Brisbane on the first morning of the Ashes three weeks later.

▦ PUMP AND SPLENDOUR

When the Australians arrived in England for the start of the 2005 tour, a Twenty20 match was arranged between the countries as a dress rehearsal for the real business of the summer. At that time, the most shortened version of the game had yet to catch on as the worldwide phenomenon it is now, and the tourists didn't take it too seriously.

England, however, had other ideas.

'We're normally slow starters and they're all about aggression,' said Gough, who played in that game at the Rose Bowl. 'Our plan was to be aggressive from start to finish. That included verbals, batting and bowling – we were told: "Don't worry about the result, just show them!"'

The Aussies were caught on the hop as England tore them apart and Gough was certain that match was pivotal in setting up the home side for regaining the Ashes, especially after his confrontation with Andrew Symonds.

Darren Gough gets ready to take on Andrew Symonds at the start of the 2005 Ashes summer.

'We all know Symonds is a big, strong lad and a tough cricketer, but you can't show you're afraid,' he said. 'When I played in that Twenty20, I bowled a short ball that hit him and I fronted up to him as if it was a boxing match and yelled "Come on then!" But it was all mental, just to show them here's their biggest "hardman", if you like, and we weren't afraid. Everybody was pumped up for that game and they didn't know what had hit them.'

▦ CAPTAINS CLASH

Another significant tone-setting moment in that epic 2005 series, which saw England finally defeat the Aussies after nearly 20 years of hurt, occurred early in the first Test.

As England captain Michael Vaughan walked out to the middle to bat, he was greeted by all manner of comments and barbs from his opposite number, Ricky Ponting. The Australian was leading his side into Ashes battle for the first time, following Steve Waugh's tenure as skipper in which he managed to win every Ashes series.

Sensing an opportunity to start afresh and put Ponting in his place, Vaughan cut the Aussie short and snapped: 'Get back to the slips, Ponting. Who do you think you are, Steve Waugh?'

A speechless Ponting did as he was told. Another strong psychological message had been sent out, so perhaps it was no coincidence that England won the series – although they did manage to lose that first Test...

▦ PARTY TIME

The Barmy Army would have been celebrating that Ashes long and hard, but they're by no means they only set of cricket fans who know how to have fun. West Indies have their Trini Posse, who occupy one stand and make as much noise as they can during every Trinidad Test match – although they tend to be slightly more musical than their English counterparts. Anybody who has ever experienced a Test on the Caribbean island will know this is the place to party. In fact, it would be easy to spend the day with the Trini Posse and forget there's even a Test match taking place in front of the stands.

To this end, England's Nasser Hussain was bang on the money when Ramnaresh Sarwan came to the crease just before lunch on day one of the second Test in March 2004. Sarwan had already made a pair in the first Test so walked to the wicket under a fair bit of pressure. As he took strike, Hussain chirped from the slips: 'Let's get this guy back to the Trini Posse Stand so he can join in the party!'

Whether it had en effect or not, Sarwan was soon on his way back to the pavilion although he managed to score 13 this time. Sadly, it's unknown whether he spent the rest of the day with the Trini Posse...

SYMONDS DRIVES KP NUTS

Sometimes the English don't quite judge the mood right with a psychological sledge and end up with egg on their faces – Kevin Pietersen knows all about that after the 2006 Melbourne Test.

The series was already lost, but England seemed to have Australia on the back foot as the hosts were five wickets down for 84 in reply to the tourists' meagre total of 159. All-rounder Symonds arrived at the crease and Pietersen announced: 'Here comes the specialist fielder.'

The Australians reserve a special place in their hearts for the man known as KP, referring to him as 'Fig Jam' which stands for 'fuck I'm good, just ask me'. There was no way Symonds was going to let Fig Jam undermine him like that. Together with Matthew Hayden, Symonds pushed Australia into an unassailable position in the match, racking up 156 in the process and England duly capitulated to lose by an innings.

Not bad for a specialist fielder.

WARNE-ING CALL

In our increasingly globalised world, word spreads fast about the latest sledging incidents and players are more than aware of what's been happening in other matches.

This was never truer than when New Zealand took on South Africa in a Test series shortly after the Proteas had faced Australia.

Daryll Cullinan had still been having problems with Shane Warne in that series, as he had throughout his career, and Kiwi wicketkeeper Adam Parore was well aware of the situation. Parore was another in a long line of especially chirpy and chippy keepers and, as he watched Cullinan fastidiously fend off the first ball he faced from gentle medium-pacer Chris Harris, he yelled: 'Bowled, Warnie!'

AN AVERAGE SLEDGE

Cullinan's South African team-mate Mark Boucher was also a wicketkeeper with plenty to say for himself – they might all share the same gene pool – and he made hay at the expense of Zimbabwe's Tatenda Taibu, another glovesman who kept quiet on this occasion.

Taibu had clearly riled Boucher and the South Africans, given the verbal onslaught that ensued: 'The only time you're looking to score runs is when you've got one seamer on the field,' said Boucher, after spinner Monde Zondeki had bowled the first ball of an over.

Taibu then played the next ball out to short mid-off only to be mocked by Boucher: 'That's a big shot, Tatenda! Where was your mouth when we were at Cape Town and we had a full seam attack?'

No such thing as a 'keepers' union between these two: Mark Boucher finally provokes Tatenda Taibu into an aggressive shot.

Once again, Taibu ignored the wicketkeeper's onslaught and allowed the next ball to drift harmlessly past his off stump. And that was the cue for Boucher to think out loud how Taibu's batting average was coming along: 'You're going to get out now because you might be averaging single figures this tour,' he ventured. 'I'll walk you to the changing room as well.'

Zondeki's next ball was fended off and Boucher went on: 'What are you averaging? You must know your average. Nine? Ten?' Still, there was no response from Taibu who had clearly decided that silence was golden on this occasion.

'Nine or ten,' continued the South African. 'I think it's nine. Or maybe it's nine point five, so we'll give you ten.'

Despite not reacting to Boucher's clear provocation, Taibu must have been affected as he was on his way back to the pavilion in Zondeki's next over – caught by Boucher.

WIN-D'OH!

The English summer of 2004 saw a poor West Indies touring side whitewashed in a four-Test series that was made memorable in sledging terms by two amusing incidents, both of which were caught by the stump mics and have since been made famous by YouTube. Both incidents also featured Andrew 'Freddie' Flintoff, which only served to enhance their status, due to the England all-rounder's global popularity.

As well as his predatory bowling and entertaining batting, it is perhaps Flintoff's famed sportsmanship that gives him the status he enjoys in the game. This was never better illustrated than by the classic moment at the end of the second Ashes Test in 2005 at Edgbaston, when England won by two runs to level the series after bowler Brett Lee had performed heroics with the bat and almost led his country to an astonishing victory.

As all his team-mates and 20,000 fans danced in delirious delight around him, Flintoff went to console the crestfallen Lee, kneeling down beside him to offer his commiserations. What could have been an opportunity for the greatest sledge of all time – when asked what he said to Lee, Flintoff has since joked: 'I put my arm around him and whispered into his ear "it's one-one, you Aussie bastard!"' – instead made the England all-rounder into a cricketing icon.

Flintoff's happy-go-lucky nature meant he was never afraid to stop play for a quick word with the opposition whether he was batting, bowling or fielding. During the first Test at Lord's, the Windies were well on their way to a heavy defeat and Tino Best was at the crease facing spinner Ashley Giles, bowling from the Pavilion End.

Flintoff and Best had previous. Earlier that year in the Caribbean, the West Indian had bowled to the Englishman without a ball, leaving Flintoff anxious that he'd lost sight of the ball and fearing he was about to be hit. It was payback time. Just as Best was getting himself set, Flintoff, fielding at slip, called out: 'Mind the windows, Tino!' and then giggled to himself.

Unable to resist the temptation, the West Indian danced down the pitch with an attempted slog and was stumped by England 'keeper Geraint Jones as Flintoff continued to giggle like a schoolchild. The only man not laughing was Best.

Tino Best fails to smash the windows, but Geraint Jones can't fail to smash the wicket – and Freddie cracked up.

▓ BRAVO LACKS BITE

Later in the series, England were well-placed when chasing 231 to win at Flintoff's Manchester home ground. The Old Trafford favourite was batting with the rather portly Robert Key, and Windies all-rounder Dwayne Bravo was getting right in Freddie's ear, encouraging his team-mate Fidel Edwards, who was bowling that particular over, that he could make a breakthrough.

'Come on Fiddy! Get the big man out, Fiddy. Come on!' clapped Bravo as he walked as close as he could to Flintoff, looking him right in the eye. 'Big man' could have referred to either himself or his batting partner, but, either way, Flintoff was having none of it and told Bravo: 'Tell you what, Dwayne. Let's see if you're around in three years, eh? Let's see where you are in three years' time. This game has a funny way of biting you up the arse. I've seen it all mate.'

Bravo said nothing and, after an awkward silence, Flintoff continued: 'I bet you won't be here.'

Unfortunately, Flintoff's warning did not come to fruition, as Bravo continued to flourish for more than three years but, by the same token, the all-rounder's attempted psychological warfare on Flintoff also failed, as the Lancastrian finished unbeaten on 57 to help his country to another victory.

▓ SACHIN MILKS IT

It would be something of an understatement to suggest that Pakistan and India don't get along particularly well on the cricket pitch – and sometimes off it too. When Sachin Tendulkar was just starting out on the road to becoming a cricketing legend, he was part of an Indian touring team playing in neighbouring Pakistan in a fairly intimidating atmosphere.

When the teenager came to the wicket, the crowd waved banners advising him to 'Go home and drink milk', but the young master showed his intentions by driving two sixes off the bowling of another young prodigy, Mushtaq Ahmed.

Abdul Qadir, who had taken Ahmed under his wing, was angered enough by Tendulkar's impudence to greet the batsman as he arrived at the bowler's end with the question 'Why are you hitting kids? Try and hit me,' to which the Indian fully obliged by carting Qadir all round the ground with four sixes and a four from his subsequent over.

He'll go a long way, that kid.

UNDER PRESSURE

Back to our old friends wicketkeepers and, in particular, Sri Lanka's Kumar Sangakkara, who once asked England off-spinner Gareth Batty 'Where's England's spinner?' while facing Batty's bowling.

He did his best to persuade South African skipper Shaun Pollock to fold under pressure during a World Cup match in 2003. When Pollock came to the crease in Durban, his country had just lost two wickets in as many balls and were still 120 runs short of victory with only five wickets in hand in a Super Six match.

Before he'd even arrived at the wicket, Sangakkara was quick to welcome him and remind him of what was at stake: 'Tons of pressure here for the skipper, yeah?' claimed the Sri Lankan. 'Gonna let his whole country down now if he fails!' he then suggested.

Pollock was unmoved and took guard from the umpire, while his opponent behind him continued to chirp: 'Lots of expectations, fellas. All the weight of all the country's expectations depending on Shaun.'

But Pollock was unfazed and managed to steer his country close to their target, although the rain-affected match actually ended in a tie.

SLEEVE IT OUT

Sangakkara was at it again when Sri Lanka played India and Harbhajan Singh came in to bat. There had been a great deal of talk about the controversial spinner's bowling action, with some observers convinced Harbhajan was bending his elbow illegally and was therefore 'chucking'.

However, the action had been deemed fit by the ICC, although the wicketkeeper was more than happy to wind up the Indian on the subject. Sangakkara noticed that Singh had arrived at the wicket in short sleeves and latched onto that with his own conspiracy theory: 'You look good in your short sleeves,' mused the 'keeper. 'Why don't you wear them when you bowl, too?' he added mischievously, much to Harbhajan's irritation.

NASSER'S NIGHTMARE

'One of the few occasions sledging worked,' is how Shane Warne described the time he managed to distract Nasser Hussain during a limited-overs international in Sydney in 1999.

England were coasting to victory in the first final of the series, and required less than five an over from the remaining ten overs, with six wickets in hand. Hussain was going well until he responded to Warne's jibe: 'This is where it's crucial not to get out, Nass. Don't let your team-mates down.'

After a bit of chat between the pair, Hussain danced down the pitch to club the Aussie for a big six and Warne applauded the shot, sarcastically adding: 'Great stuff, Nass. That's the way to do it.'

Hussain was wound up and, in a misguided attempt to speed up England's victory charge, he again marched down the wicket looking for a big hit, missed and was stumped by Adam Gilchrist. Incredibly, that sparked an England collapse and the Aussies won by ten runs.

WAGGING THE TAIL

Unlike most cautious and focused batsmen, Warne was not overly concerned about opening his mouth if he felt the time was right. As a general rule, the bowlers do most of the talking, but Warne was not your average player.

During a 2005 Ashes Test, Warne was batting at number eight and England felt they had the Australians on the rack. Andrew Strauss, at silly point, tried to rally his team-mates and rile the spinner by saying: 'Come on, guys. We're down to the tail now, let's get this guy out.'

Not only did Warne turn to Strauss and reply: 'I don't know why you're saying anything, mate. You are useless!' but he also promptly waltzed down the wicket to clump the next ball for six.

▦ WARNE IN A SPIN

Of course, sometimes Warne's verbal jousting could have quite the opposite effect and he'd come a cropper. When Australia were playing South Africa at Perth in December 2005, Warne was enjoying a spell of domination over the batsman Justin Kemp, who couldn't pick any of the Aussie's vast array of deliveries. Sensing he had his opponent on the ropes, Warne tried to get into his head and said: 'They're leg spinners, Justin!'

Justin Kemp gets his own back on Shane Warne to keep his rival quiet for a good ten seconds or so.

WHY ARE YOU SO FAT?

Remarkably, Kemp managed to fend off Warne, but was still cheaply dismissed by Glenn McGrath. In the hosts' subsequent innings, Warne was batting after his team-mates had piled on the runs, but he fell for only five – to Kemp, of all people.

Even though the Aussies were in a strong position, Warne was still unhappy and his misery was compounded when he passed Kemp and the South African said: 'They're called inswingers, Warnie.'

▦ BIG MAC STRIKES BACK

Another South African who had trouble deciphering Warne's spellbinding bowling was all-rounder Brian 'Big Mac' McMillan. According to former captain Mark Taylor, the Aussies had decided not to sledge the burly South African during the 1994 Test series, essentially because of his size. But Warne couldn't resist.

After another bamboozling spell of bowling, McMillan looked dumbfounded and Warne seized the moment, saying: 'Hey, Big Mac! I'll call them out to you – maybe that'll help.'

Amazingly, as the Aussie sent down each delivery he called 'wrong 'un!' or 'flipper!' or 'leg spinner!' and each time, McMillan still failed to put willow on leather. By this stage, he was extremely frustrated and the hulk of the man came bounding down the wicket to Warne at the end of his next over and said: 'Hey, Shane! You're coming to South Africa next month. Hundreds of people go missing or die in our country every day. Another one won't make any difference.'

Warne turned white at McMillan's threat and when he bowled his next over, he'd lost all his rhythm and sent down a series of full tosses. An alarmed Taylor went to check what was the matter with the star bowler and all Warne could utter was: 'Do you think he meant it?'

▥ GUNNING FOR BORDER

'Big Mac' was at the centre of an astonishing moment during that subsequent Australian tour of South Africa, when he told visiting captain Allan Border that he was going to shoot him after the close of play one day.

Nobody had really paid any attention to McMillan, but the Aussie dressing room was stunned into silence when the bulky all-rounder burst in after stumps that evening brandishing a handgun and asking where Border was.

Everybody pointed in the direction of the captain, who was sitting by his locker, and parted as McMillan walked slowly and purposefully towards Border, gun in hand. As he reached the bench where the 38-year-old Australian was sitting, McMillan sat down, put the gun next to him and pulled a can of Castle out of each pocket.

'Fancy a beer?'

▥ URINE NO POSITION TO SLEDGE ME

Sometimes, an attempted sledge is met with such derision that the subsequent retort is far more memorable than the original half-baked insult. That was certainly the case for Australian Simon O'Donnell during a match against India when he attempted to unsettle the great Sunil Gavaskar.

The thought-provoking jibe was so unmemorable that it hasn't emerged unscathed through the annals of history but Gavaskar's response certainly did. He instantly rounded on the bowler and said: 'No need to sledge me. I've been sledged more times than you've had pisses.'

▦ MAKING A SPECTACLE

Trent Bridge, 4 June 1964 – the first time a 23-year-old dogged Yorkshire opening batsman made an appearance in a Test match arena. His name was Geoffrey Boycott.

It was the first Test of the summer and England's opponents were Australia. As Boycott and Fred Titmus made their way out to the middle, the Aussies took a good look at the bespectacled debutant and hatched a plan to unsettle him. And it wasn't the most sophisticated piece of tactical cricket ever devised either.

As Boycott took guard, visiting captain Bobby Simpson and his bowler Garth McKenzie were locked deep in conversation that was just loud enough for others to hear: 'Hey, Garth!' said the skipper. 'Look at this four-eyed fucker! He can't bat! Knock those fucking glasses off him straight away!'

Although that uncultured bit of psychological banter has been widely reported ever since, to this day Boycott claims he never heard it: 'I've no recollection of that at all. As far as I'm concerned I never heard it – maybe he told him that privately? They were wasting their breath on me. It didn't even go in one ear and out the other; it just didn't go in. I was like Bjorn Borg, the tennis player. We were very similar. When he went on court and I went in to bat, we were both switched on. If my mum had been speaking to me or the Queen of England, it wouldn't have made much difference.'

As if to prove the point, Boycott was clearly unaffected that day as he hung around for two-and-a-half hours and top-scored with 48 in England's meagre first-innings total of 216. And McKenzie never did knock his glasses off.

▦ STATE OF EMERGENCY

English cricket's greatest rivalry is the Roses match between Yorkshire and Lancashire, so-called as each county sports a different coloured rose as its emblem. The animosity dates back to the War of the Roses, an altogether more serious and bloody affair than the cricket matches between the counties. However, one bowler was determined for a return to the good old days of fifteenth-century warfare during a Roses County Championship match in the early noughties.

Yorkshire bowler Steve Kirby, him of the earlier run-ins with Steve Waugh, was a latecomer to first-class cricket who more than made up for lost time by developing a reputation for sledging and competitiveness. Ironically, he was born in Lancashire, but that counted for nothing when Lancashire leg-spinner Chris Schofield arrived at the crease and prepared to face Kirby.

'Around the wicket, umpire,' instructed Kirby. 'And call an ambulance!'

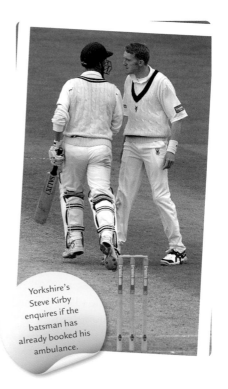

Yorkshire's Steve Kirby enquires if the batsman has already booked his ambulance.

A ROUGH WELCOME

With mind games, the earlier the doubt is cast, the better the chances of success. Like Kirby, the Australians have been known to be keen to try to muddle an opponent's head before they've even given them the courtesy of facing a ball.

During the 2002 tour of South Africa, the Aussies gave promising young batsman Graeme Smith a torrid time at the start of his Test career. The 21-year-old, coming in at the fall of the first wicket, hadn't even arrived at the stumps for his debut in the second Test at Newlands, when Matthew Hayden began taunting him: 'You're not fucking good enough,' said the Aussie. 'How the fuck are you going to handle Shane Warne when he's bowling into the rough?'

Smith didn't have to worry about Warne, as he was quickly back in the dressing room with just three runs to his name thanks to Glenn McGrath. He underlined his immense potential in the second innings with a fluent 68 before being caught behind – off the bowling of Warne.

THE SOUND OF SILENCE

Possibly one of the most audacious attempts at psychological torture on a cricket pitch has to be England's 1997 self-imposed gagging order on themselves. Having realised that Australian batting machine Steve Waugh relished a sledging confrontation at the crease, it was decided by coach David 'Bumble' Lloyd and skipper Mike Atherton that no England player would say a word to Waugh while he was at the crease during the Old Trafford Test.

'If you get into Steve Waugh, it makes him play better,' recalled Lloyd. 'We had a plan that we wouldn't say a word to him.'

With England 1-0 up in the series after two rubbers, this was to be a pivotal match. And, as the Aussies languished on 42 for three when Waugh arrived at the crease, England scented blood and put their plan into action. It didn't take Waugh long to twig something was up: 'Oh, I get it. Nobody's talking to Steve. OK! I'll talk to me fucking self!'

Amazingly, Waugh spent the next four hours chattering away to himself while compiling a typically dogged 108 out of his team's total of 235, before repeating the trick – both with his bat and his mouth – in the second innings with 116 as Australia romped to victory. The series was to follow.

▦ DROPPING A CLANGER

A sledge that has always been attributed to Waugh but seems to have been, at best, exaggerated or, at worst, a fallacy was when he was dropped by South Africa's Herschelle Gibbs during the epic 1999 World Cup semi-final. Waugh was supposed to have said: 'You've just dropped the World Cup,' but has since denied this.

But, a very similar incident occurred two years later in the second Test at Kolkata between India and Australia, a match that immediately became a candidate for the greatest game ever played.

After being forced to follow on, India posted a huge second innings score to set the Australians 384 to win. The game seemed to be petering out into a draw, with the tourists on 161 for three at tea on the final day. Shortly before that final break, Sourav Ganguly put down a difficult chance that would have removed Waugh and given the Indians a sniff of victory. Realising his good fortune, Waugh turned to the Indian skipper and gloated: 'You just dropped the Test, mate.'

But, straight after the interval, the Aussie captain was dismissed by Harbhajan Singh and as he departed, Rahul Dravid called out: 'Who's given the Test away now?'

He was right, as Australia collapsed to 212 all out and India went on to win the series in the third Test. And, in his book *Ground Rules*, Ganguly admitted how much Waugh's comment had changed the game: 'Maybe if he had said nothing, the game would have drifted to a draw, the result that appeared to be its natural conclusion. But Waugh could not resist the chirp... Sometimes sledging can work against you and, on this occasion, it had the effect of geeing up the Indians.'

▦ THAT'S KAIF!

Former England captain Nasser Hussain never missed an opportunity to score sledging points or to try to gain an advantage for his team – but with mixed success. His presence on the field was a noisy one and he didn't just confine his mental attacks to the batsmen either.

When England were playing India in a one-day tournament (which also featured Sri Lanka) in 2002, Sachin Tendulkar was flaying the bowling to all parts of Durham's Riverside ground on his way to making a century. But Hussain was niggled by the perpetual presence of India's Mohammad Kaif, who kept appearing in the middle with various gifts for Tendulkar. From several changes of batting gloves to drinks and even a cap, Kaif was on the pitch for almost as long as the England fielders and it irked Hussain.

On one of these trips, the players were called off for a rain interruption and as Kaif trudged off with everybody else, Hussain let rip: 'Hey you, what are you? Sachin's bag carrier or something? What do you do for this team? Who are you?' Kaif replied with some choice words for Hussain and that was seemingly the end of the matter.

However, nine days later, the teams met again in the competition final at Lord's. Everything was going England's way with the visitors 116 for five, chasing 327 to win, halfway through their innings. But, that was the moment Kaif came in to bat.

No doubt with Hussain's words still ringing in his ears, the Indian bludgeoned an unbeaten 87 off 75 balls to steer his side to victory and Ronnie Irani, who was playing that day, remembers it well: 'Every time Kaif hit a good shot, he'd look over at Nasser and Nasser was just fuming. Why on earth he opened his gob is beyond me – he cocked it all up!'

BORN TO SLEDGE

With wicketkeepers playing such a prominent role in this chapter, it's fitting to end with a mini-tribute to one of English cricket's barmiest and most talkative men behind the stumps, Paul Nixon.

Known as 'Nico', he's a cricketer who takes his role as a wicketkeeper extremely seriously, believing he is in a position to make things happen. 'A wicketkeeper can have the last comment,' he explained. 'He can be right next to the batsman just before they start their physical and mental routine. So if someone can just say something at the last minute that makes a difference, if anybody can do it, it's the 'keeper.'

After years on the county cricket scene in England, Nixon was finally given his international nod at the age of 36 for a one-day series in Australia in 2007. And the chirpy chappy wasted little time in trying to wind up every Aussie who stood in front of him for long enough.

'Duncan Fletcher [the England coach] asked me to be vocal and strong and in the Australians' faces,' explained Nixon. 'We'd just been outplayed in the Ashes and we needed a new impetus. First and foremost we had to play good cricket.'

In the final of that series, Andrew Symonds was batting and Nixon knew him from playing together for English county side Kent. 'I said to him: "Symo, when you nick it to me, I'm going to send you a signed scorecard every day for a year," and about three balls later he nicked it to me!'

The crazy 'keeper is well aware that he must reap what he sows, but that does not bother him one jot: 'You've always got to know that if you do give it a bit, you're going to get a bit back as well. For me, I quite enjoy it as it gets me going a little bit if somebody is a bit more vocal towards me.'

That was certainly the case when the entire Sri Lankan team waded into him during a World Cup match: 'Sri Lanka, as a unit, were unbelievable. Every single one of them was like a man on a mission. Normally in a side you only get it from one or two and that's about it. But with Sri Lanka, it was coming from every direction with things like: "What are you doing here?" or "You're useless!" or "Where's your bus pass?" or "Are your parents still alive?"'

During that World Cup, Nixon enjoyed what was probably his finest hour behind the stumps thanks to an inspired plan that accounted for West Indian Marlon Samuels.

After appearing on cult British TV show *Soccer AM*, the 'keeper was told about a darts player who used to put his opponents off by asking them whether they tended to breathe in or out when they released each dart. He was encouraged to repeat the trick on the cricket pitch and he tried it with Samuels.

'I said to him: "Do you know when the ball is bowled and you're about to hit it, do you actually breathe in or breathe out?" and he sort of looked at me as if to say "Are you for real?" The next ball he smacked it to mid-wicket to Paul Collingwood. To be fair, he hit it that hard he nearly broke Colly's hand.'

The breathing trick seemed to have come up trumps, but Nixon modestly remained uncertain: 'Who knows if it worked or not?'

All this begs the question, has anyone ever managed to shut up this veritable budgerigar of a chirpy wicketkeeper? And the answer is yes, way back in the early days: 'My first-ever sledge that I can remember, Steve Waugh was at silly mid-off when I was playing against Australia for Leicestershire in an Ashes warm-up match. I played and missed and Waugh said: "Fuck me, mate. What time does the proper fucking cricket start?" And I was like: "Oops! I'm doing my best here."

'Any batsman like Graham Gooch or Des Haynes that you sledge to get them off their game and they then go on to make big hundreds – that shuts you up more.'

Batsmen of the world, there you have it. All you have to do to shut Nixon up is score runs. Simple!

PAUL NIXON

Perhaps modestly, Paul Nixon's stand-out sledge is based around an incident that occurred early in his career and featured a couple of his Leicestershire team-mates.

During a County Championship match, Leicestershire were bowling and some of the effort in the field wasn't quite what it should have been. Gordon Parsons was trying his heart out with the ball, while his fellow paceman Les Taylor was patrolling the third man boundary.

'We used to call Gordon Parsons "Head of Semtex" because he was like a highly explosive substance,' chuckled Nixon.

And the Head of Semtex was pretty browned off when he saw Taylor fumble a routine piece of fielding and give away a boundary.

'A few overs later, the same thing happened but vice-versa,' recalled Nixon. 'Gordon fumbled a ball which went for four off Les's bowling. And Les bawled at him: **"Come on! What are you doing down there at third man? You're absolutely useless!"**

'Gordon said: **"Les, what's four more when you've gone for twenty-five thousand?"**'

As his team-mates guffawed with laughter, Taylor realised his over-reaction and meekly admitted: **'Actually, yeah, you're quite right!'**

Despite Nixon's modesty in selecting one of his colleagues' sledges as his pick of the bunch, he received the ultimate accolade of his own following his tour Down Under

in 2007. Instead of being riled by this gobby, old has-been who'd had the cheek to dish out abuse to their heroes, the Aussie fans were delighted to see an English player playing with such attitude – and wrote to Nico to tell him: 'The reaction and fan mail I got from Australia was unbelievable,' he explained. 'They'd enjoyed an Englishman coming over and giving the Aussies a bit back.'

Having said all that, Nixon is still certain that his Australian counterparts have still not become fully accustomed to being sledged: 'The Aussies like to give a bit, but they're terrible at taking it.'

Paul Nixon, a man who can always rise to the occasion when a bit of sledging is called for.

CHAPTER FIVE

ANATOMY OF A SLEDGE

What are the vital ingredients of a good sledge? In this section, thanks to the help of a few people who've played the game at the highest level and indulged in a spot of banter themselves, it's time to take a proper investigative look at this unique cricketing phenomenon. **It's not exactly the science behind sledging, but it's probably the closest we'll ever come to understanding what it's all about…**

▦ WHY SLEDGING?

Ironically, even the origins of sledging are a source of argument. Ian Chappell and many other Australian cricketers believe the term originated from a team-mate who swore in the presence of a woman and was described as being as subtle as a sledgehammer. From then on, any vulgarity on the pitch was shortened to a sledge and so it went from there.

However, a rival school of thought tends to point to a specific incident in the 1960s when a New South Wales bowler came in to bat during a match. His wife had allegedly been having an affair with a team-mate so, as he approached the wicket, the opposition began to sing Percy Sledge's hit single 'When A Man Loves A Woman'. This type of banter became known by the artist's surname and thus sledging was born.

Whatever the origins and whoever was right, the banter or psychological warfare between opponents that became known as sledging had been going on for more than a century, as the W.G. Grace anecdotes in this book demonstrate. In fact, it's a fair bet that when the cavemen stopped using their long pieces of rock to bash each other over the head for a moment or two, and started to bash tiny stones with them instead, they were probably sledging each other too.

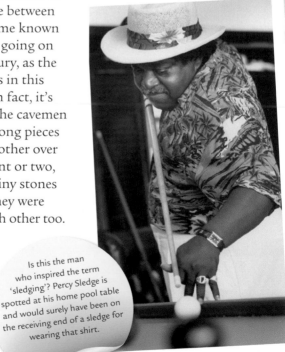

Is this the man who inspired the term 'sledging'? Percy Sledge is spotted at his home pool table and would surely have been on the receiving end of a sledge for wearing that shirt.

MENTAL DISINTEGRATION

Australian captain Steve Waugh coined the phrase 'mental disintegration' to make sledging sound a great deal more clinical and scientific than a load of blokes dressed in white swearing at each other. But, in essence, he was right. Sledging isn't just about being rude or abusive – although it does help. The tactic is specifically designed to undermine and distract opponents and therefore induce mistakes.

By and large, it's batsmen that are the target of almost all sledges. One mistake costs a batsman his wicket, so if that can be encouraged through a little psycho-babble, bowlers like Shane Warne would be mad not to give it a go. As the great man himself has said: 'If I can get a batsman out by saying something that affects his game so much, then why not?'

One person who would most certainly take issue with that theory is former England captain Geoffrey Boycott, who believes sledging is tantamount to cheating. When interviewed for this book, he pulled no punches in his assessment: 'My view is there's no place for it, but that's my view. If the bowlers can't get batsmen out by fair means why should they try something else? What they're saying is on pure ability they're not capable of getting people out. They're trying to get another advantage and I think it's a slightly unfair advantage.'

HOW TO SLEDGE

It seems that, by a country mile, the most important ingredient in any sledge is humour. Ask anyone that's ever played the game and they will all tell you, anything funny is perfect, but anything too abusive is unacceptable.

But not all cricketers are comedians. David Lloyd recalled a Test match in Australia when he was in charge of the England team during which Stuart MacGill, fielding at point, attempted to have a quick word with one of the tourists. But Steve Waugh was unimpressed with MacGill's comment and rebuked him by saying: 'Look, if you're no good at it, just keep your mouth shut!'

Luckily, however, there are some amusing characters out there, or this book would have fast become a pamphlet. Former England fast bowler Darren Gough was one of the mainstays of the side throughout the 1990s and early noughties and he contributed more than just wickets.

'I'm not really into sledging,' explained Gough. 'My main thing is to be sharp, quick-witted and try to make it funny, just drop the batsman's guard. There is the odd time when it can get personal and aggressive, but it very rarely happened with me.'

But the Yorkshireman was a firm believer in adapting to situations, rather than having a cheeky remark already hidden up your sleeve before taking the field. 'It's better to be spontaneous,' he said. 'Otherwise you get these bad sledgers who stare you down and then say something as they're turning away. What does that do? Most of the Australian fast bowlers tend to be like that, not many of them say anything face to face.'

Gough locked horns with Glenn McGrath on many occasions during his career and he was still uncertain about the methods of the paceman who finished his stint with an astonishing 563 Test wickets.

'The thing with Glenn McGrath is that you never knew if he was speaking to you,' pondered Gough. 'Because he used to chunter to himself, sledging was a way of winding himself up so a lot of people didn't know if he was sledging them or sledging himself. You never knew.'

Gough's former England limited-overs international team-mate Ronnie Irani was unequivocally clear about how to sledge and why: 'It's got to have a humour side to it,' he said. 'You've got to make people laugh or smile, because it's all about making them lose concentration so you can get them out. It's not about getting one over on them from a verbal point of view, it's about actually getting them out.'

Some players are known for giving the impression that verbals count for as much as anything else. Kumar Sangakkara has built up an unhealthy reputation for sledging from behind the stumps for Sri Lanka, but he has gone on record to pledge that he has always been honourable: 'The Sri Lankans are determined to be as tough as anyone on the field,' he said in an *Observer* interview. 'We have tried to be tough, both mentally and physically, but not dirty. It is nice to have a clean, wonderful game, but it does not always work out like that. Sledging is part of the game. As long as it is not vindictive that's OK – and it helps if it's humorous.'

And the wicketkeepers' union maintain the same line through former England gloveman Paul Nixon, who preaches exactly what he practises on the pitch. 'What I try to do is try to make them focus on something else and not about the game. I try to get into their heads so they get cheesed off with me or angry with me. I'll hit a nerve if I can but try not to get personal.'

▦ HOW NOT TO SLEDGE

If humour is the essential ingredient of sledging, then, as Nixon pointed out, personal jibes are strictly off limits in the war between the wickets. It's one thing having a joke about the batsman's poor technique, but it's quite another to make crude suggestions about their wife's, ahem, technique.

David Lloyd, a former umpire as well as player, coach and commentator, argued there was still a role for officials to play when sledging goes too far: 'If it's personal and vindictive, the umpire has to step in but the majority of it is banter and good fun. If it's nasty and personal there's no room for it – it's very cheap and cowardly. But the majority of the stuff you can just have a laugh about.'

And Lloyd was equally adamant about how a batsman should best deal with being the sledgee, as it were: 'You're better off saying nowt when you're batting and getting them back when you're fielding.'

Current international umpire Simon Taufel seemed to back up Lloyd's message when he once explained that the limits of sledging for him were: 'Once it broaches personal issues and once it sort of supersedes your moral boundaries of what language is tolerable. Most umpires will tend to let the players get what they want to say off their chests and, from our perspective, we'd rather make it a player versus player issue rather than a player versus umpire issue.'

Former England all-rounder Chris Cowdrey also lamented the advent of the more abusive sledging that has permeated its way from

WHY ARE YOU SO FAT?

the professional game through to junior cricket: 'The idea of sledging was to distract the batsman, it wasn't to be abusive and I see a lot of school and club stuff where players are just abusive to the opposition. There's nothing funny about it and there's nothing clever about it. They are not actually trying to put them off their game but they are just being aggressive because they think it's clever. It's childish really.'

Even renowned sledger Nixon has his limits: 'I would never talk about families. Moeen Ali, who plays for Worcestershire, has a fantastic, big beard. When he played at Grace Road, I kept talking about split ends in his beard. It's more fun and banter. I'm not sledging him for having a beard or anything, far from it. It's anything I can get a reaction to that'll hopefully get him off his game for a ball or two.'

talkSPORT's veteran cricket correspondent and former player Jack Bannister believes sledging has become a significantly worse problem over the years due to the sport's exposure to modern media: 'I played in a different era when sledging wasn't so common. There were very few people who didn't walk when they were out. There was less press coverage, not so much money in the game and not so many TV cameras there.'

But the new breed of international players is definitely aware of the negative impact of sledging and how it should be used. England's giant paceman Steven Finn has said: 'It's important you don't get too emotional. It can cloud your thinking and if it's too obvious, the batsman knows he's winning.'

Worcestershire's Moeen Ali sports a little extra chin protection.

▦ WHO TO SLEDGE

So having worked out how to sledge effectively and the etiquette behind it all, the most crucial aspect that's left is which players to target. And it would seem that any player who will answer back with a smile on their face is probably the least likely person to be affected by a sledge.

'It's all about the character and the individual,' said Irani. 'Some people are a bit more reclusive and don't like it, so you can go at them hard. If somebody came at me aggressively, swearing and being abusive, it made me play better and concentrate harder. I thought: "I'll show you. Don't you talk to me like that." Generally, I wouldn't answer anyone back because, as a batsman, you only get one chance.'

But the former Essex star admitted he could sometimes have to psyche himself up with a bit of old-fashioned aggression when he walked to the wicket. 'Sometimes I felt I needed to fire myself up a bit and be aggressive – and that was before I'd even faced a ball. I remember doing it once when someone in the Pakistan team hurled abuse at me from the moment I'd come through the gate until I was at the crease. So I turned round and said: "Who are you talking to, you haven't got a run all series!" That made me concentrate harder as I thought to myself: "You can't afford to get out here or you will really cop it." All that abuse kind of helped me.'

In other words, don't bother sledging Irani or any other equally combative characters – just pick on the weak. And some players are not worth wasting words on either, purely because they're not good enough, according to self-deprecating Zimbabwean one-hit wonder Eddo Brandes: 'I never really heard too much when I was batting, because I'm not sure if I was good enough to receive sledges,' he said.

'Some players are more susceptible to it. Players work out who will falter – it's about establishing weaknesses. I heard a lot of tales from our top-order batsmen. They said Steve Waugh was really subtle and clever from gully – McGrath and Warne were always at it. They would all make comments that had nothing to do with cricket but would get the batsmen thinking about other things.'

One batsman who never thought about anything other than what was happening on the 22-yard strip in the middle of the pitch was Boycott. Aside from his disdain for the practice, he also claimed he was never affected by any comments on the pitch.

'It's not something that's bothered me because I just didn't listen when I played, I just switched off,' he said. 'I had the ability to concentrate and to switch off, I suppose that's handy because nothing ever got to me and therefore I didn't get involved in any altercations or eyeball staring.'

Boycott also suggested that sledging was just another way for competitive men to wage war on one another and that was another reason why his was a lonely existence out in the middle.

'Some men think that it's a macho thing to stand up to each other, or it's an ego thing, but it never bothered me. I didn't get involved, so I actually didn't get very much. Looking back, if people see that they can't upset you, I suppose they feel like they're wasting their breath, they're wasting their time and they're wasting their energy, aren't they? For me, it wasn't a big deal and that's why I didn't get very much.'

So, definitely don't bother sledging Boycott under any circumstances, nor several other England captains, including Andrew Strauss. The current skipper has enjoyed enormous success as an opening batsman since entering the Test arena, especially against Australia.

This could be due to his attitude to the banter: 'Sledging's not a big thing for those of us that play cricket a lot of the time,' he said. 'If you're going to get affected by sledging then you probably shouldn't be out there in the middle in the first place.'

And Strauss also has little time for pacemen who think they are intelligent for creating original sledges: 'Bowlers always try to think up some new ones – it usually takes them about six months to come up with anything.'

Another former Middlesex and England captain, Mike Gatting, shared a similar view of the Australian obsession with sledging: 'I didn't actually notice them [Australians] sledging me to be perfectly honest,' he once said. 'They say a few things at the beginning just to settle you in, but for me it was never really anything to worry about. They only sledge people who they think it might affect.'

England's pace ace Stuart Broad was another player who believes most words out in the middle are wasted – refreshing for a bowler, although he remains keen to establish himself as an all-rounder so perhaps not as refreshing: 'They are only words, aren't they?' he has claimed. 'You don't get much in the county game, but I spent a winter playing in Australia after I left school and got barraged because of my old man [Chris Broad] doing so well over there. That was a great learning experience, it toughened me up.'

So, essentially it seems weak-willed batsmen are the perfect sledging sitting ducks – as long as they're not West Indian, according to Cowdrey: 'West Indies have always just got on with the game, played and backed themselves to win. OK, they are not doing so well at the moment, but they just play cricket. They never sledge.'

Is it acceptable to sledge a woman? England's Clare Connor and Australia's Belinda Clark believe it would be rude not to...

Lastly, and most significantly, is it right, or even acceptable, to sledge a woman (within the context of cricket, of course, rather than just verbally castigating an innocent female passer-by on the street)? Sledging is rife in the women's game, with England and India falling out during a recent series and players close to tears.

England skipper Clare Connor has said: 'Women cricketers can get very personal and very crude. It happens in rugby, football and all other international sports, so why should cricket be any different?'

But women's cricket pioneer and former England captain Rachael Heyhoe-Flint would beg to differ as she holds a far more traditional view of how the sport should be played – by both sexes: 'Cricket is supposed to be a quiet game with good manners,' she commented. 'Sledging is not in the traditional spirit of the sport. It is appalling and damaging to cricket's image. A lot of it is just imitating the men's game.'

To sum up, it's best not to sledge anyone who is West Indian, relishes the chance to answer back or happens to be a woman with a double-barrelled name over the age of 50. Anyone else is fair game and bound to be ripe for a bit of mental disintegration.

▦ THE FINAL WORD

Most observers believe it's healthy and good for the game for sledging to continue. Former cricketer and cricket TV analyst Simon Hughes said: 'I think it's actually important, because I think you want to see if there's emotion in the game. Competitive sport is compelling to watch because emotions become involved, so I don't like to see players have to contain their emotions totally. I think a few words here and there can be entertaining, funny and interesting.'

But, Boycott stands typically firm and resolute that there is no place for any chat between bowler and batsman in cricket. 'It's not a part of the game which I like or of which I approve,' he said. 'I don't think there's any need for it. I know some players think that it's part of the game to try and upset a batsman so he loses concentration, and it's a test of their mental strength and their character. I don't think that way – I think you can play sport pretty hard within the letter and spirit of the laws but without that.'

RAVI BOPARA

Like many West Indian players, Viv Richards was not the biggest sledger – especially when he was concentrating on knocking the leather off the ball out in the middle. He was a man who preferred to let his cricket do the talking. When he wasn't leading the Caribbean side to victory all over the world throughout the 1980s, Richards could be found plying his trade for English county side Somerset and it was during a match with Glamorgan that he uttered some of the most immortal words in sledging history.

Certainly, according to England and Essex batsman Ravi Bopara: 'To be honest, I'm not a massive sledger,' said Bopara. 'I never really sledge, but the best one I've heard about is Viv Richards v Greg Thomas.'

Thomas was a bit-part England paceman, who spent most of his career with the Welsh county. During this particular match, he was enjoying some success against the Windies legend and, probably in a moment of poor judgement because he could scarcely believe the success he was having, he decided to put the boot into one of the game's greatest batsmen.

Having seen several of his deliveries go whistling past Richards' flailing bat, Thomas sarcastically told the batsman: **'It's red, round and weighs about five ounces, in case you were wondering.'**

As with so many great comedy moments, it doesn't matter how predictable the joke is nor for how long you can see it coming – there is still plenty of joy to be had to see

MY FAVOURITE SLEDGE

the moment played out. And that was exactly the case the moment Thomas uttered his cocky words.

He walked back to his mark, ran in hard, bowled the next ball and was soon looking way into the distance as Richards hammered the red and round thing not just for six, but out of the ground and into an adjacent river. As Thomas's skywards gaze turned back towards the batsman, Richards calmly reminded him: **'You know what it looks like, now you go and find it.'**

Viv Richards hits another six for Somerset against Glamorgan on his way to a 48-ball hundred while his cap attempts to defy gravity.

CHAPTER SIX

WHEN VILLAGE GREENS GO BLUE

From club cricket in England to the Grade game in Australia, the amateur side of the sport is the perfect breeding ground for sledgers everywhere. And for those who don't manage to make the step up to the next level, there's still plenty of fun to be had from dishing out abuse to all and sundry without having to worry about being picked up by a stump microphone. Thanks to a network of spies, moles and tell-tales from a Third XI near you, here's a look at some of the best banter from cricket's unsung heroes.

■ BUMBLE'S SIX APPEAL

The Lancashire League is well known as an extremely tough breeding ground for future stars of the game, as well as a home for the best amateurs. Former Lancashire and England star David Lloyd returned to play for his hometown club Accrington when he'd already turned 60, and received a predictably hostile reception from opponents.

Having been an England coach and subsequently an extremely popular Sky Sports commentator, 'Bumble' still retained a huge enthusiasm for the game, but that meant nothing to the Lancashire League regulars. And in a match against Todmorden, Lloyd had to summon up his old sledging powers:

'We were on a really difficult pitch against Todmorden – the wicketkeeper had been giving me loads [of stick] and the off-spinner came on. If I could do anything, I could hit off-spinners. Anyway, I hit him over the boundary wall, and in the same over I did it again. I turned to the wicketkeeper who had been on my case and said: "Go and ask him what it's like to be hit for six by a pensioner."'

■ MUMMY'S BOY

Although Ronnie Irani became an Essex stalwart, his cricketing education was also in the no-nonsense Lancashire Leagues, where he was schooled from a very young age.

He explained: 'In club cricket, things were tough. Senior blokes used to sledge you, telling you how bad you were and how good they were. I became used to it. It's just how Northerners in the Lancashire League are. They're aggressive and they'll let you have it. Someone once asked if my mother was still ironing my whites for me. You don't bother replying to that when you're thirteen – and it helped me later in the game not to respond to it.'

HIT FOR SIX

If the Lancashire Leagues are tough, it's even harder in Grade cricket in Australia where sledging has turned into physical violence. Western Australia club Melville, once the home of Dennis Lillee in his formative years, were the team that had shame brought upon them.

Michael Fishwick, an old friend of Leicestershire and England's overly talkative wicketkeeper Paul Nixon, was the man who lost his cool. 'Nico' takes up the story: 'Somebody was swearing at him while he was batting and I'm not sure whether he dropped his bat or threw his bat at him, but he then flew at him and punched him. He got banned, obviously.'

Obviously.

PATIENCE IS A VIRTUE

Occasionally, top international players pop up to play in Grade matches in order to warm up for the season or loosen up after injury. When Australian fast bowler Geoff Lawson was playing in one of these games, he was bowling to a notoriously slow Indian player who began to aggravate him.

Do not keep this man waiting. Shoaib Akhtar grimaces in pain as Geoff Lawson works on his ankle after Akhtar turned up 84 seconds late for practice.

Each time Lawson bowled, the batsman would play his best forward defensive stroke and yell 'Waiting!' to his partner at the bowler's end. After one block and 'Waiting!' call too many, Lawson snapped: 'Mate, you're not the only one. The whole fucking world's waiting!'

▦ LOW BLOW

Canberra club cricket doesn't have as brutal a ring to it as a Sydney or Melbourne Grade game, but that wasn't the case for young batsman Rob Badman. Badman, still in his late teens, was facing an extremely hostile and aggressive bowler, who could probably give Andre Nel a run for his money in the in-your-face stakes.

The batsman made the mistake of playing one too many streaky shots off the fast bowler, who marched down the wicket and bawled: 'You're living up to your surname. Although Completely Shitman would be more accurate.'

Instead of replying, the somewhat overawed youngster pretended to do some pitch gardening and set himself up to face the next ball, a predictable bouncer which he promptly carted through midwicket for four.

As several opposition team members began to laugh, the bowler's face reddened and he positively steamed in with the next ball, which squared 'Completely Shitman' up and thudded into his private parts. But that wasn't enough for the bowler, who then stood over his fallen prey, mullet blowing in the wind, and yelled: 'Bleed, you little prick! Bleed!'

▦ CASTING A SPELL

Grade cricket bowlers are a special breed and do a fine line in aggression and pace, usually combined. They don't, however, usually think through the consequences of their sledging.

Once, a quickie was trying his heart out and, having hit the batsman on the pads several times, was not getting the decision.

He walked down the wicket and said to the batsman: 'Mate, do you even know how to spell lbw?'

Undeterred, the young batsman said little and simply pulled the next ball for six. As the bowler watched the red thing disappear into the distance, the batsman asked him: 'Mate, do you know how to spell six?'

BARBADOS BOUNCERS

When Bunbury cricketing legend David English was on tour with the Southern Drifters in the Caribbean, he was forced to learn the local rules the hard way. Like their professional counterparts, the West Indian amateurs were not overly keen on being sledged, so when Barbados bowler Stamford Clarke Jr was busily marking out his unusually long run-up, he wasn't best pleased to hear English interrupt him.

The batsman had finally lost patience after watching the bowler walk 40 yards from the stumps and he bellowed: 'I don't go that far on my holidays!'

Predictably, the bowler zipped his first ball past English's nose at 90mph and suggested that he 'smell the leather, man.' And, even more predictably, a brave knock from a helmet-less English ended in hospital where he required stitches after being felled by another Clarke Jr bouncer.

LOST PROPERTY

London's Middlesex County Cricket League has long been a breeding ground for some of the England team's biggest names, including Mike Gatting. But, it's the unsung heroes and characters of this league that are worthy of mention.

Teddington's opening bowler Richard Ballinger, a former England Under-19 player, was locked in a battle with Winchmore Hill's opening batsman Nad Mohammad. Both players were exchanging the usual pleasantries like 'you're shit' and 'go fetch it', which was pretty much run-of-the-mill Saturday afternoon fare.

After Mohammad played two glorious flicks through midwicket for fours, he attempted the hat-trick, but instead saw his off stump cartwheeling along the ground towards the slip cordon. Instead of celebrating the dismissal, Ballinger never broke stride after his follow-through and continued running all the way to the slips, picked up the stump and then chased the batsman back towards the dressing room, shouting: 'You're missing something, aren't you? Is this yours?'

▦ BOLD PREDICTION

Another Teddington bowler made a name for himself in a match against Brentham, although this time he was lucky to escape in one piece. One of the Brentham batsmen was proving to be a particularly stubborn sort and wasn't playing many shots. Despite provocation from the bowler along the lines of 'Are you going to play a fucking shot today?' the batsman remained calm and blocked his way through several overs.

But the bowler eventually wore him down with a steady cascade of abuse until the batsman replied: 'Just fucking bowl. You can't get me out.'

Like a red rag to a bull, the bowler screamed for the ball that was being passed through the field, waved it in front of the batsman's face and said: 'Right, this fucking ball, you are out, you c***! Look at it carefully. This fucking ball, you're out!'

Sure enough, the bowler produced the perfect inswinging yorker that rapped the batsman's pads and the umpire raised his finger. This cued an extraordinary celebratory jig where the bowler slid on his knees in front of the batsman, screaming: 'Fuck off, you're out! Didn't I tell you?' and the square leg umpire had to intervene to separate the players.

For the remainder of the innings, however, the bowler was forced to move to the slips from his usual fielding spot on the boundary at fine leg due to several threats of extreme violence from the vanquished batsman.

⊞ GOOD 'EVANS!

Richmond's left-arm spinner, nicknamed 'The Penguin', is something of a legend of the Middlesex League. He has played in the competition for more than 30 years and is a unique figure with his distinctive, public school, posher-than-posh accent, which he is never afraid to use on the pitch.

During a local derby match, The Penguin induced a top edge from a batsman who was attempting to sweep and, as the ball was on its way to square leg, he decided to celebrate early.

'You're out!' he shouted at the forlorn batsman. 'Shit shot, now sod off.... Oh no, hold on a minute. Evans is under it...'

As he spoke those words, Evans duly dropped it and The Penguin sighed: 'Why is it always Evans?' Possibly, the only occasion where a cricketer has managed to sledge both a team-mate and an opponent without pausing for breath.

⊞ TWO GOOD

Perhaps The Penguin's most endearing, spectacular and legendary moment in the Middlesex League came in a tight contest against Winchmore Hill. The spinner was bowling, with the opposition requiring only five more runs to win but in the perilous position of being eight wickets down. As the number ten batsman arrived at the crease, he asked the umpire: 'How many balls are left in the over please?'

Before the official had a chance to part his lips, The Penguin bellowed: 'Two. One for you and then one for the next fucker!'

He promptly dismissed the number ten and eleven batsmen to win the game for his side and walked off the pitch muttering darkly.

NEVER GO BACK

Darren Gough is certain the sledging and banter is far more intense in club cricket than in the international game – and he's not even safe going to watch his son play. 'It's worse when you go back to local leagues,' said the former England player. 'If someone hits you for four, people watching from the other team give you abuse like "Oh, you're rat's pace, you're over the hill, you're crap." It's not the ones who are playing against you; it's the ones who are already out.

'I went to watch my boy play and he got out, and this man came up to me and said: "That's made my day that, my lad getting your son out." I'm thinking: "What are you telling me that for?" Somebody's got to get him out. He's twelve! For him, it meant the world to get my son out. So it's still going on now and I've retired.'

 ## BARMY BRAVADO

Not so much a sledge, but an incredibly brave show of confidence with a good smattering of stupidity – that would describe the incident when Andy Caddick opened the bowling for a Somerset XI against Millfield School in the early 1990s.

Having just qualified to play for England, Caddick was hoping to find some rhythm and form in the pre-season warm-up game. The Millfield openers that day were Alistair Dalton and Ian Ward, who would go on to play five Tests for England. As future Glamorgan player Dalton took strike, he watched Caddick hurtling in off his long run. Before he'd had time to register, the bowler had sent a lightning fast bouncer skidding past Dalton's nose.

With audible gasps all around the field, Dalton immediately turned to the pavilion, removed his helmet, signalled for the twelfth man to come and retrieve it and said as loud as he could: 'No need for this, absolute rat's pace!'

▓ INTRODUCTION RUCTION

Although outbreaks of violence still remain rare, the threats sadly remain, but sometimes with hilarious consequences. During a Middlesex League match, one batsman who was being sledged to the point of insanity claimed he was on the verge of walking off the pitch, going to his car and returning with a shotgun if it didn't stop.

On another occasion, a player who was fairly new to the league was at the crease, but had made a habit of running straight down the middle of the pitch. After patiently watching the batsman contravene the rules for far too long, a genteel veteran behind the stumps made an extremely polite request to the umpire to be alert to it. The batsman immediately took offence, telling the wicketkeeper to 'Fuck off! Who do you think you are?'

At that point, a close fielder confronted the batsman and said: 'I don't know who you are, but this guy has been playing in the league for thirty to forty years. Don't speak to him like that.'

'You don't know who I am?' replied the batsman. 'I'll introduce myself to you in the car park later. I've done GBH, me.'

The stunned fielder could only offer: 'Well, I've eaten at GBK.'

▓ BUM DEAL

Just like their counterparts in the professional game, amateur wicketkeepers are not overly fond of silence. An Australian batsman was playing one of the innings of his life during a Grade game but was not being allowed to enjoy the moment too much by the parrot in pads, standing behind his stumps.

This wicketkeeper had not shut up from the first ball of the batsman's knock and, as he passed his double century, was still on permanent rabbit mode. Finally, the batsman snapped, turned to the wicketkeeper and said: 'Listen mate, you're shit. As long as your arse faces the ground, you're never going to play State cricket!'

▦ COMMON DECENCY

Back in the Middlesex League and, due to a quirk of the fixtures, Brondesbury and Hertford were playing each other on consecutive Saturdays. There was a little bit of needle between the teams after controversial incidents in previous matches, so when Brondesbury managed to dismiss their opponents for just 70 in damp conditions while playing at home in the first game, Hertford were clearly a little miffed.

With the home team coasting to victory on 50 for one, the Hertford captain began a monologue about the conditions. 'This place is a disgrace,' he said. 'Next week, at our place, we'll have a decent outfield, a decent pitch, decent sightscreens and a decent lunch.'

'Yeah,' replied the home skipper. 'But are you planning on bringing any decent players?'

▦ TEXTBOOK CRICKET

In one of Brondesbury's Sunday fixtures, they found themselves up against a team made up of West Indian expats, whose batsman was struggling. After one of a series of streaky edges through backward point, the home captain grew frustrated and said: 'I wonder what page of the MCC coaching manual that comes from?'

Almost predictably, when the skipper brought himself on to bowl his off-spin a couple of overs later, the same batsman managed to execute the perfect cover drive for four. With his elbows still up and holding the pose perfectly, he looked up at the bowler and, in his Tony Cozier-style Jamaican accent, said: 'MCC coaching manual, page one!'

▦ HIT AND MISS

In another local league game, a batsman was having terrible trouble connecting with the ball and the fielding team were only too happy to add to his misery. Each time he missed, he'd be sledged with lines like

'This bloke couldn't hit the water if he fell out of a boat', and after one false swing too many, the wicketkeeper said: 'Mate, just fuck off would you? You clearly can't play and you're just boring us all.'

Finally, the batsman reacted to the mounting pressure and turned to the 'keeper with his bat raised and said: 'If you don't shut the fuck up, I'm going to hit you with this bat.'

'That would be the only fucking thing you've hit all day,' was the 'keeper's instantaneous response, as the sounds of hysterical laughter rang around the pitch.

The scene may be picturesque and the cricket gentle-paced, but league and village cricketers can always match their Test counterparts at one thing: sledging.

CATCHES WIN MATCHES

Club cricket umpires are also happy to get in on the sledging act whenever possible. In one game, where a tense finish was on the cards due to a number of dropped catches, a loud and convincing lbw appeal was turned down by the official. At the end of the over, the captain approached the umpire and said: 'Come on, that was plumb. Any danger of us getting a decision?'

The umpire was in no mood for such insolence and replied: 'If you bastards could catch, this game would be over by now.'

▦ HEADING FOR TROUBLE

Bowlers are not known for being overly sympathetic towards batsmen, and this was illustrated perfectly in a Lancashire League game. When a batsman arrived on a fast, bouncy wicket minus his helmet, he was strongly advised by the fielding team to protect himself. Foolishly, he insisted he knew what he was doing and was happy with his decision.

It wasn't long before a bouncer had crashed into the side of his head and he was lying on the floor next to the stumps. The bouncer's bowler walked down the wicket, stood over the batsman to see blood pouring from his ear before pronouncing: 'Will someone get this c*** a helmet?'

▦ MAKING THE GRADE

Tom Simpson was an English batsman looking to spend a winter in Australia improving his game by playing Grade cricket. In his first match, he found himself selected to play for the fifth grade team, which mainly featured older gentlemen and plenty of youngsters.

Simpson was determined to keep a low profile, mindful of how giving away his English roots could lead to an uncomfortable day's action. So he began by calling for his runs quietly until he'd made around 20 or 30 and was starting to feel more confident in his new surroundings.

As he dispatched the next ball firmly towards the boundary, he called out a much louder, brasher and altogether English-er 'Yeah!' to his batting partner and crossed.

'Hang on a minute,' said a fielder. 'We've got a Pommie. You're a Pommie aren't you, mate?'

'Yeah,' replied Simpson.

'Long way to come to play fifth grade, isn't it?' asked the Aussie, as only Aussies can.

DAVID LLOYD

One of cricket's most famous commentators, David 'Bumble' Lloyd has called some of the great Test and limited-overs games over the last decade. He's also coached England at home and abroad and played international cricket too. But for his favourite sledge, Bumble nominated a game with which not too many people would be familiar: the Lancashire League fixture between Accrington and Haslingden. That would seem a strange choice until you consider Lloyd was playing for Accrington at the time.

'I had just made a comeback at the age of sixty-one,' he explained. 'I said to myself before "I know I'm going to get heaps here, but I ain't saying a word."'

Although Lloyd hadn't played in his local league for many years, he was well aware of the kind of characters he would be facing – at best, there would be minimal respect for who he was. At worst, he was going to be subjected to a fearful battering of sledging and intimidation. He was not to be disappointed. And he was also not to be true to his pre-match declaration.

'I went out to bat and got a fearful amount of stick,' he said. 'It was literally minutes long. Then, this lad at short leg came up with the final insult. He said: **"You were no fucking good twenty-five years ago and you'll be no fucking good now!"**

'I walked across to him and said: **"You obviously know who I am. I've got no fucking idea who you are!"'**

In the absence of a coin, rival captains David Lloyd and Geoff Boycott prepare to toss an umbrella before a Roses match at Bramall Lane, Sheffield.

Despite being retired for many years, Lloyd's sledging is not just confined to the local leagues. Thanks to his work in the Sky Sports commentary box, the former England coach never misses an opportunity for a cheap shot from behind the microphone. Once, during an England tour of Sri Lanka, Lloyd was calling a Test at Kandy when the camera zoomed in on our old friend Arjuna Ranatunga, who was looking larger than ever. Lloyd couldn't help himself as he informed the watching millions: 'Is that Ranatunga? Strewth, he's not missed many lunches, has he?'

CHAPTER SEVEN

ONE-HIT WONDERS

This isn't just the place for the sledges that didn't really fit anywhere else. Although it is that too. But, mainly, these encounters are memorable because of their unique nature. Either the sledger wasn't a prolific mouthy sort, as featured elsewhere in the book, or the actual utterance was unlike anything that has gone before or since. **These are the one-offs and we salute them for their individuality. All of them...**

▦ FAMILY FEUD

The fifth Ashes Test at The Oval in 2001 had nothing riding on it. Australia had already won the series convincingly. But this was the Ashes, and there is no such thing as a dead rubber. Especially when it comes to Australian sledging.

After piling on more than 600 in their first knock, the Aussies had England on the back foot at 313 for seven, still 328 runs behind, when debutant bowler Jimmy Ormond came to the wicket. Having taken one for 115 in Australia's innings, he'd hardly set the world on fire and slip fielder Mark Waugh, brother of captain Steve, was quick to let him know it.

'What the fuck are you doing out here?' asked Waugh. 'Surely you're not good enough to play for England?'

'Maybe not,' replied Ormond. 'But at least I'm the best player in my family.'

No matter what he achieved on the pitch – he played in only one more Test – it hardly mattered because, with that riposte, Ormond guaranteed himself a place in cricket folklore.

James Ormond celebrates taking an Ashes wicket – and being the best player in his family.

SINGER-KKARA

Whacky wicketkeeper Kumar Sangakkara also grabbed a place in cricket folklore with a bizarre moment during a Test match against England at Kandy. It's one thing jabbering away from behind the stumps, but singing to a batsman is quite another, so this is more than likely the only incident of its kind.

Nasser Hussain was under pressure as England captain at the time and the Sri Lankan's way of making that point was to burst into song when the Englishman arrived at the wicket.

'Bye bye love / Bye bye happiness / Hello loneliness / I think I'm going to cry,' he warbled at a completely bemused Hussain. Unlike the Everly Brothers, Sangakkara's truly was a one-hit wonder.

SEXY CRICKET

Arguably trumping the Sri Lankan's singing was an ingenious stunt pulled off by England wicketkeeper Steve Rhodes during an Ashes warm-up match against New South Wales.

A fortnight before the Test series in 1994-95, Aussie Michael Bevan had allegedly enjoyed a hotel room tryst with a particularly vociferous and enthusiastic female companion. Somehow, a tape recording of this illicit rendezvous had made its way into Rhodes' pocket while he was keeping wicket.

When Bevan came to the crease, Rhodes timed his pressing of the 'play' button to perfection and, as Phil Tufnell skipped to the wicket to bowl, the batsman was utterly horrified and confused to hear something that sounded like an all-too familiar blue movie coming from behind him. It wasn't long before Tufnell had claimed Bevan's wicket.

▦ FROM ZERO TO HERO

It's strangely satisfying and reassuring to know that Viv Richards could also sledge as well as he could bat. The two skills don't always go hand in hand, but Richards was certainly up there with the best in the sport's essential skill-sets – and he'd do both in as cool, calm and collected manner as possible. All while nonchalantly chewing on a piece of gum.

Back in late 1983, during a West Indies tour of India, he clashed with home legend Sunil Gavaskar, who was also no shrinking violet. The Windies were romping away with the six-match Test series and they led 3-0 going into the final game at Madras. Gavaskar had been opening the batting for his country throughout the series, but decided to move himself down the order to number four for the dead rubber.

After the Windies had posted a first-innings total of 313, Gavaskar didn't have to hurry off the pitch as usual to pad up – or so he thought. Malcolm Marshall had other ideas. The fearsome paceman removed opener Anshuman Gaekwad and number three Dilip Vengsarkar without troubling the scorers, meaning Gavaskar came to the crease with two wickets down and no score on the board.

As he made his way to the wicket, Richards strolled over to him and remarked: 'Man, it don't matter where you come in to bat – the score is still zero!'

As a footnote, Gavaskar managed to maintain his composure, despite Richards' provocation, as he struck a Test-best unbeaten 236 to ensure India earned a draw.

DON AND DUSTED

Not all sledges take place out in the middle – in fact, one of the very best occurred in the dressing room after a day's play. They all count.

When Australia were trying – but failing – to vanquish the invincible West Indies side of the 1980s, they enjoyed an excellent day's cricket at the Adelaide Oval in February 1989 in which even bowler Merv Hughes helped himself to an unbeaten 72 out of a total of 515. As was the way back then, players from both teams were enjoying a few 'cold ones' after the game in the visitors' dressing room when in walked Sir Don Bradman, who was keen to meet the all-conquering Caribbean kings.

Each West Indian stood and waited to meet arguably the greatest cricketer of them all – except bowler Patrick Patterson, who remained seated until Bradman approached him. The paceman seemed puzzled and as he rose to his feet, he looked down at the small, frail 80-year-old and said: 'You, Don Bradman? You, Don Bradman? I bowl at you, I kill you man. I split you in two!'

'You couldn't even get Merv Hughes out,' replied Bradman. 'You'd have no chance against me, mate!'

CLOSE BUT NO CIGAR

Brian Close could never just be out. The Yorkshireman was as adamant as one could be that if the umpire's finger was raised, there would always be extenuating circumstances to explain the dismissal.

During the 1970s, he captained a Somerset side that included the young Peter Roebuck. By then, Close was well into his forties but his outlook on the game, and getting out, had never changed. Roebuck had opened this particular innings and could only look on as his team were reduced to four wickets down with just 11 runs on the board. The captain was next in and, as he arrived in the middle, he asked Roebuck how the pitch was behaving.

'It's absolutely swinging all over the place,' replied the young opener.

'Right,' said Close. 'We're in the shit because of shit shots so no more shit shots, right?'

Roebuck nodded and returned to the non-striker's end where he watched Close fend off two balls then advance down the wicket to attack the third, only to be caught at mid-off. Roebuck could barely make eye contact with Close as the skipper walked past him on his way back, but the captain caught his eye anyway and shouted: 'You said to me it was swinging, but you didn't tell me it was seaming as well!'

▦ THE SPIRIT OF CRICKET

Aussie all-rounder Shane Watson will forever be haunted by a Darren Gough sledge at the Riverside in 2005. During the limited-overs international series, the tourists were staying at Lumley Castle in Durham, where legend has it that a ghost still walked the building at night.

Watson was so spooked by the rumours that he spent the night sleeping on team-mate Brett Lee's floor, a story which Gough was quick to exploit once word had got out.

When Watson was at the non-striker's end, Gough crept up behind him and did his best Scooby-Doo ghost impression by raising both arms in the air and hanging them over the batsman.

'It was just one of those things that I did,' says Gough. 'I don't know why I did it. I said: "Don't worry, Shane. You can sleep in my bed tonight!" People in the crowd thought it was funny and he had a chuckle too.'

▦ HUSSAIN'S A HOOT

Nasser Hussain's oversized nose was a sledger's dream. During Australia's Ashes warm-up match against Essex, Hussain's hooter came under attack with an effort that sits nicely alongside Ian Healy's 'three-mile radius' gag catalogued earlier.

On this occasion, Healy instructed fielder Stuart Law to position himself 'right under Nasser's nose' and, upon hearing this, Law began walking to the boundary. He kept on going all the way back to the ropes before turning round and yelling: 'Fuck me! The ground's not big enough, mate!'

Darren Gough, who was playing for Essex in that game, recalled how the whole ground had enjoyed the moment: 'We all got that one – that was class. It carried around the ground and we all chuckled. Even Nasser laughed and that was a rare thing.'

For Hussain, it was just another in a long list of nose-based insults, but he was more than capable of dishing it out too, according to Gough.

'Nasser would really get personal. He was a very strong character and was not afraid of upsetting anyone; he wasn't there to make friends. He tried to intimidate the Indians, Pakistanis and Sri Lankans, because he used to get a bit off them with him being of Indian descent. He used to get really stuck in, but he also used to get a lot of stick as well – especially about his hooter.'

▦ DONALD'S LAMB STEW

When two South Africans clash the results are often special and the two Allans, Donald and Lamb, didn't disappoint in an English county match. Lamb was born in South Africa but played his international cricket for England, a fact which was not lost on Donald as he steamed in to bowl.

The batsman played a front-foot shot and missed, so Donald suggested: 'Lamby, if you want to drive, go hire a car!'

The next ball, the same thing happened as Lamb moved his feet and swished the bat in an attempt to connect, but with the same result – an air shot. 'Lamby,' continued Donald. 'I told you: if you want to drive, go hire a car!'

It was third time lucky for Lamb in the next ball, as his sweet strike saw him drive effortlessly through the covers for a boundary. He looked up at Donald and said: 'Hey, AD! Go and park that one!'

ON THE MAKE

When is a sledge not a sledge? When it's a blag. If that sounds confusing, allow Sky Sports commentator David Lloyd to explain what happened when England players were picked up attempting to snaffle free luxury goods on the stump microphone in a Test against Pakistan.

'I remember when Matt Prior got into a little bit of trouble for saying: "What sort of watch have you got?" on the stump microphone. He also asked: "What sort of car do you drive?" which sounded very demeaning to the Pakistanis.

'But it was totally innocent. He wasn't talking to them. He was talking to Alastair Cook and was asking him those questions. He was then answering "What I'd really like is one of them Breitlings" or "I'd really like a Rolex – that's a cracking watch."

'It was all to do with some company, possibly beer, that was mentioned by one of the players on the stump mic, so they sent the team a case of it. So then the players thought "I wonder what will happen if I mention that I'd like a Rolex watch?" Unfortunately, it was interpreted as being demeaning to the Pakistani team, but in fact they were just on the blag on the stump mic!'

A BARD LESSON

If you're an English batsman, there's only one thing worse than a fired-up, Australian fast bowler. And that's an angry, fired-up, Aussie fast bowler. When Australia were playing a tour match against Leicestershire in 1989, tail-ender Jonathan Agnew made the mistake of showing some resistance in a failing cause – with both his bat and mouth.

Geoff Lawson was wound up with Agnew's continuing presence at the crease and unleashed a beautifully paced, four-letter-word-filled rant at the batsman. Agnew, retaining an angelic expression, enquired: 'Is that Shakespeare, Mr Lawson?'

Before he knew it, 'four balls in succession were wrapped around his ears' – according to his batting partner Paul Nixon – and he eventually capitulated to be caught by Allan Border. Off Lawson, of course.

HAVING THE BALLS FOR IT

Another English cricketer who capitulated was Tony Greig when he was outwitted by young David Hookes in the Centenary Test, played at Melbourne in 1977. The 21-year-old was batting number six for the Aussies in a tight match and Greig, England's South African-born all-rounder, who still spoke with a Springbok accent, tried to seize the chance to take advantage of a young kid on debut: 'When are your balls going to drop, sonny?' he enquired.

Hookes, completely unintimidated, replied: 'I don't know, but at least I'm playing cricket for my own country.'

As if that wasn't enough, shortly after, Hookes hit five consecutive fours from Greig's off-spin as he helped give Australia enough of an advantage to go on and win the match. Years later, before his sad and untimely death at the age of 48, Hookes wryly observed about that Melbourne incident: 'I made Tony Greig famous.'

▦ TWO OUT OF THREE AIN'T BAD

Going back even further, it has become increasingly fashionable among cricketing elites to dismiss the advent of sledging as a modern illness that is detrimental to what is traditionally viewed as a gentlemanly sport. But the founding fathers of cricket were at it as much as their descendants are today.

The bearded batting sensation W.G. Grace was involved in one particularly memorable exchange – not that anyone is around today who could possibly remember this far back. Even Richie Benaud.

In a late nineteenth-century county match, Essex quickie Charles Kortright, the fastest bowler of his era, was having considerable success against Grace, although the umpires didn't seem interested in any of his appeals. Undeterred, Kortright continued to steam in and finally clean bowled 'The Doctor' with a humdinger of a delivery that left two of Grace's three stumps in a nasty mess.

The legendary batsman stood his ground for possibly a moment too long in the vain hope that the umpire might save him with a no-ball call and, as he finally trudged off with his bat tucked under his arm, Kortright remarked: 'Surely you're not going, Doctor? There's still one stump standing!'

▦ MARSHALL LAW

On the subject of one stump standing, the West Indies were once the most feared team in world cricket. Their famous and fearsome bowling attack which, over time, consisted of Colin Croft, Joel Garner, Michael Holding, Andy Roberts, Malcolm Marshall and others took on all-comers and there was usually only one winner.

By and large, the bowlers let their cricket do the talking – usually by sending round bits of leather flying past batsmen's noses at speeds of 90 mph or more. Sledging wasn't necessary for the Windies attack and there are not many recorded instances of the Caribbean quickies attempting to undermine players with verbals.

Admittedly, Holding could lose his temper, and he once kicked down the stumps in protest at an umpire's decision during the highly controversial 1979-80 Windies tour of New Zealand. But, like Marshall, Holding was more likely to intimidate batsmen with his bowling.

The lightning-fast Marshall did once have words with Australian David Boon, who'd made the poor decision to play and miss consecutive deliveries from the West Indian: 'Now David, are you going to get out now or am I going to have to bowl around the wicket and kill you?'

▦ TESTING TAUNT

With its all-Australian cast, the Sheffield Shield is a fantastic breeding ground for the country's future Test players – and sledgers. Sadly, not everyone makes the grade and one of the country's best players never to play Test cricket was South Australia's Jamie Siddons, who went on to become a coach at international level instead.

During a Shield game against New South Wales, Siddons was fielding at slip when Mark Waugh arrived at the crease. Most players take guard from the umpire, do a spot of gardening to remove any unwanted debris from the track and settle down to face their first ball.

On this occasion, however, Waugh took a great deal longer. He took three different guards from the umpire and just when it seemed he was about to take strike, he wandered away to study the leg-side field placings. Finally, he returned to the stumps and took guard from the umpire again.

This was all too much for Siddons who barked: 'For fuck's sake! It's not a fucking Test match!'

'Of course it isn't,' replied Waugh. 'You're here.'

TWELFTH ANGRY MAN

Usually, a substitute fielder, more often than not the twelfth man, wouldn't involve himself in any kind of banter with the opposition. After all, he would hardly be in a position to do so having not even been picked to play in the match. Apparently, this rule does not apply to Australian twelfth men.

Indian all-rounder Ravi Shastri was once batting against the Aussies at the Sydney Cricket Ground when he looked to take on a quick single. But, as the ball arrived in the hands of sub fielder Mike Whitney, Shastri hesitated. Whitney aimed to shy the ball at the stumps and said: 'If you leave the crease, I'll break your fucking head.'

An infuriated Shastri replied: 'If you could bat as well as you can talk you wouldn't be the fucking twelfth man.'

DRIVING THE POINT HOME

One twelfth man who could definitely bat as well as he could talk was Justin Langer, but he failed to spoil Nasser Hussain's moment in the sun in 1997's first Ashes Test at Edgbaston. It was a rare game of 1990s Ashes cricket where everything went right for England, having reduced Australia to 54 for eight on the first morning. Even the sledging was spot on.

While Hussain was compiling a gargantuan innings, the Aussies replaced bowler Jason Gillespie with sub fielder Justin Langer, and he joined in with the general banter and abuse that had been coming Hussain's way. Except that was not acceptable for the England batsman who, as Gough indicated, enjoyed a confrontation.

'Look, I don't mind the others chirping at me, but you're just the bus driver of this team,' snapped Hussain at Langer. 'So you get back on the bus and get ready to drive it back to the hotel this evening.'

Hussain went on to score 207 as England won by nine wickets – it was definitely one of the better Test matches for the so-called Poms.

AN ENGLISHMAN IN SYDNEY

As a graduate of a top grammar school and Cambridge University, Mike Atherton was never going to endear himself to the in-your-face Australians. A clash of cultures was inevitable, and so it proved when Atherton first joined England on an Ashes tour in 1990-91.

Going into the third Test at Sydney, Australia were already 2-0 ahead and England were firmly on the ropes. And, after seeing the Aussies post 518 in their first innings, the situation seemed even more hopeless. But Atherton played one of his typically obdurate innings to stifle the Australians and helped himself to a century in the process.

In the early part of his knock, the opening batsman survived a justified appeal for caught behind and wicketkeeper Ian Healy was livid. Unsurprisingly for Healy, he let Atherton have it, walking past the batsman at the end of the over and telling him: 'You're a fucking cheat!'

As calm and composed as he could be, Atherton quietly turned to Healy and said: 'When in Rome, dear boy...'

CHASING YOUR TAIL

Occasionally, bowlers don't engage their brains before spewing out of their mouths whatever has come into their minds. And that can leave them wishing they'd never bothered in the first place.

On an Ashes tour in the 1990s, Australian paceman Paul Reiffel was doing his best to mop up the tail of an English county side. Dismissing a number eleven shouldn't have been cause for too much concern, but having seen the hapless batsman play and miss once too often for his liking, Reiffel couldn't help but observe out loud: 'You're the worst batsman I've ever seen.'

To which the bemused county man replied: 'I'm number eleven. What did you expect?'

BLUE BROTHER

There's probably only one thing worse than the difficulties associated with having a famous sibling. And that's the difficulties associated with having two famous siblings. Just ask Dean Waugh, younger brother of Australian legends Mark and Steve. Dean had to be content with a more modest career, plying his trade in Grade cricket. But nobody ever let him forget his more successful brothers.

Once, during a Sydney Grade game between Gordon and Bankstown, Waugh was at the crease, struggling badly against former New South Wales bowler Richard Stobo.

Time and again, Waugh played and missed (it's not often those four words are printed) until Stobo could no longer resist: 'Mate, are you fucking adopted?'

SREESANTH'S GOT TALENT

Not so much a sledge, but more a piece of performance art. Take a bow, Shanthakumaran Sreesanth. As the Indian fast bowler stepped out to bat in Johannesburg during the 2006-07 Test series against South Africa, he was given a warm greeting by effervescent Springbok paceman Andre Nel.

The South African is no stranger to controversy, having pushed the boundaries of the whole sledging thing as far as they can go, sometimes too far, resulting in suspensions. Nel welcomed Sreesanth by telling him: 'I can smell blood. You do not have the guts.'

Having seen Nel very deliberately move the field around, Sreesanth knew some short-pitched bowling was coming and Nel didn't disappoint. And he continued to bait Sreesanth, at one point fingering his nation's emblem on his shirt and saying: 'I am playing for this. You are a scared fellow, rabbit. I will get you next ball.'

But, he couldn't have been further from the truth as Sreesanth clubbed Nel's next ball straight back over the bowler's head for a huge, majestic six. Lost in a moment of sheer triumph – and no doubt, relief – the Indian then ran down the pitch alongside

Nel while twirling his bat round and round above his head and performing some kind of wonderful, rhythmic gyrating dance move that would not have been out of place in a Bollywood nightclub: Sreesanth 1 Andre Nel.

Andre Nel caught in a rare conciliatory pose while Sreesanth warms up for his audition to become a Bollywood nightclub cage dancer.

▦ NERVES OF STEELE

The element of surprise can often produce hilarious moments on the cricket pitch. And so it proved when England gave a shock call-up to Northamptonshire batsman David Steele for the 1975 Ashes Test at Lord's. What was most notable about Steele, other than his glasses, was his full head of grey hair, which made him look closer to fifty-three than his thirty-three years.

Whether it was nerves or plain incompetence is unclear, but Steele actually managed to get lost on his way down to the pitch from the Lord's dressing room, ending up in the basement. When he eventually made it out to the middle, Aussie bowler Jeff Thomson was waiting for him with a smirk on his face as he studied the unusual looking sportsman.

'Who's this, then?' asked Thomson. 'Father fucking Christmas?'

But Steele was partial to the odd sledge himself as, rumour has it, when he finally arrived at the crease that morning, after taking his guard he turned to wicketkeeper Rod Marsh and said: 'Take a good look at this arse of mine, you'll see plenty of it this summer.'

And he was right. Father effing Christmas made 50 and 45 at Lord's and went on to enjoy a sparkling summer without a failure of note. The *Sun* described him as 'The bank clerk that went to war' and he even won the BBC's Sports Personality of the Year award for 1975.

▦ OLD WIFE'S TALE

Phil Edmonds was not your average cricketer. He was equally concerned with his business interests as well as donning his whites and would often turn up to county and Test matches in his Rolls Royce.

His Middlesex colleague Simon Hughes was more fearful of him sledging his own team-mates than an opposition batsman: 'He didn't have much to say to the batsmen. He had a go at his fielders more often.' That said, Hughes also recalled one memorable sledge: 'When Geoff Boycott was just blocking, Edmonds would chirp: "You'll never die of a stroke, Geoffrey."'

Edmonds had a famous wife, the author Frances Edmonds, and that proved to be his undoing, in sledging terms, during an Ashes Test. Australian wicketkeeper Tim Zoehrer, who had come in for a barrage of abuse from Edmonds, replied to him: 'At least I have an identity. You're only Frances Edmonds' husband.'

☷ IN YOUR SHOES

Staying in Australia, another remarkable Ashes Test was played at Adelaide in December 2006. England racked up 551 for six in their first innings before declaring and leaving the Australians an awkward nine overs to negotiate before the close of day two. When captain Freddie Flintoff had Justin Langer caught in the second over, his counterpart Ricky Ponting decided to put himself in at three for the remaining overs rather than send in a nightwatchman.

Freddie Flintoff makes one of the least successful sledges of all time, just after England have made 551 for six in Adelaide. Ricky Ponting made 142 and Australia won the Test.

Flintoff immediately seized on this possible error of judgement and started laying into Ponting: 'I wouldn't like to be you if you get out here.'

Matthew Hayden was at the bowler's end and, on behalf of his skipper, put the ball firmly back in Flintoff's court with: 'I wouldn't like to be you if we win from here, mate.'

It turned out to be a strangely prophetic counter-punch, as Ponting scored 142 in Australia's reply of 513 before England were dismissed for just 129 and Australia knocked off the runs for an unlikely win late on day five.

▦ WATER SHORTAGE

One of the fiercest Australian captains of all was Allan Border. He was a no-nonsense man who ran a tight ship. At the start of an Ashes tour in 1993, he told journalists: 'I am not talking to anyone in the British media. They are all pricks.'

And when he wasn't winding up the press, he was reserving his best lines for whichever English cricketer was getting on his nerves. After overseeing two Ashes defeats to the old enemy in 1985 and 1986-87, Border was in no mood to make it an unwanted hat-trick in 1989. By the time the teams arrived at Trent Bridge for the fifth Test, the Aussies had already claimed the urn as they were 3-0 up. But that didn't stop Border being any more competitive.

After Australia had amassed more than 600, England were toiling with the bat, although Robin Smith was playing a typically defiant innings. On his way to a century, Smith had the audacity to request a drink during a session, much to Border's chagrin.

'What do you think this is, a fucking tea party?' bawled Border. 'No, you can't have a fucking glass of water. You can fucking wait like all the rest of us.'

Was that a no to the water, then?

MAMMA MIA!

A cricketer never knows when a joke, sledge or seemingly innocuous comment may come back to bite them on the backside. Like elephants, it seems certain cricketers never forget. When Ian Botham returned from a tour of Pakistan in the 1980s, he joked during an interview that he wasn't overly keen on the destination, claiming 'Pakistan is the sort of country to send your mother-in-law to.'

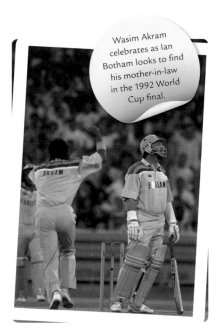

Wasim Akram celebrates as Ian Botham looks to find his mother-in-law in the 1992 World Cup final.

The comment did not go down well over in southern Asia but, like most storms in teacups, pretty soon it had blown over and everyone got on with playing cricket. Then, when Pakistan and England met in the 1992 World Cup final, Botham was out for a duck as England's run chase began in the worst possible way.

And there was Aamer Sohail, ready to add insult to injury, as Botham departed: 'Why don't you send your mother-in-law out to play, she can't do much worse.'

BREAKING UP IS HARD TO DO

Banter between the wickets is considered fair game by many as long as it doesn't become personal – and even then, it's fine if it's funny, apparently. During a 2005 limited-overs international between England and Australia, Kevin Pietersen was getting on top of Shane Watson's bowling. The Australian all-rounder was not having a particularly good time on the tour. Haunted hotels aside, most troubling for him was that he had recently separated from his dancer girlfriend Kym Johnson.

After Pietersen blasted the Aussie for a huge six, Watson unleashed a volley of abuse at the English batsman, who replied: 'You're just upset because no one loves you any more.'

Kevin Pietersen's advice to Shane Watson to check out some online dating sites didn't go down too well.

If the TV pictures were anything to go by, Watson stormed off to field at square leg while, amazingly, Pietersen shared the joke with Ricky Ponting and Damien Martyn, who could both be seen smirking.

▦ WHO CHUCKED ALL THE PIES?

One exchange in which Pietersen definitely ended up on the losing side was a sparring session with Indian all-rounder Yuvraj Singh. The pair are firm and committed rivals on the pitch and exchanged words during both Test matches of England's tour to India in 2008.

During the second Test in Mohali, while Pietersen was compiling a handy little knock of 144, he was heard by the stump microphone telling Yuvraj: 'You're a cricketer not a god, Yuvraj. Concentrate on your batting, you'll play a bit more. I'm a little bit tougher than you are, brother.' As Pietersen talked, Yuvraj sarcastically pretended he'd been shot by holding his belly.

Later, in that evening's press conference, Pietersen was asked about the rivalry between the two. 'He's got me out a couple of times and I'm his so-called bunny but he's not good enough to call anyone his bunny,' said the England skipper. 'I'd rather face a pie-chucker like him all day than Zaheer Khan with the new ball.'

It seemed Pietersen was well ahead on points, but Yuvraj held court at the following evening's media gathering and began by saying: 'Relax, the pie-chucker is here. They told me it [pie-chucker] meant I was a useless kind of a bowler, so it shows KP hates getting out to me – getting out to a useless bowler five times is quite useless batting, I would say.'

▦ COLD CALL

Our old friend Steve Kirby must have saved his best lines for Roses matches, as he was at it again with a sledge that was as memorable as it was utterly obscure. Kirby was pumped up for one particular County Championship match against Lancashire, especially to be bowling against former England captain Mike Atherton.

Not only did he come out on top in his duel with the Lancastrian by dismissing him in both innings, he also found time to tell him: 'I've seen better players in my fridge!'

▦ DESPERATE MEASURES

From one cricketing rivalry to another, and the Indian tour of Pakistan in spring 2004 in which Indian batsman Virender Sehwag smashed an incredible 309 in the first Test at Multan. Understandably, the Pakistan bowlers became increasingly irate at being unable to dismiss Sehwag, with Shoaib Akhtar leading the way. The 'Rawalpindi Express' sent down a series of short-pitched balls but, instead of hooking as Akhtar hoped, Sehwag simply ducked underneath them.

As Akhtar became more desperate, he began to encourage Sehwag with a series of overstated hand movements that looked like hook shots. At this point, the normally ice-cool Sehwag tired of the bowler's antics and said to Akhtar: 'Are you bowling or begging?'

Even the bowler's team-mates saw the funny side of that one.

SIMON HUGHES

Merv Hughes is something of a modern-day sledging phenomenon. Humour was never far from his lips – and not just in the shape of his exceptional moustache – and his namesake Simon argues his finest hour came in an Adelaide Test match between Australia and Pakistan.

' I wasn't involved in this one,' said the former Middlesex bowler whose solid county career never quite translated itself into any international appearances. 'But, it's great fun, although it may have been exaggerated over time.' Let's not dwell on that thought too long as we go back to South Australia in 1990.

The tourists were batting with the fiery Javed Miandad at the crease, a man whose controversial past was well known to the Aussies. Back in 1981, Miandad had become embroiled in an on-pitch spat with Australian Dennis Lillee in which he had to be stopped from whacking the bowler with his bat by umpire Tony Crafter – this, after Lillee had kicked him.

There was nothing gentlemanly about that unsavoury incident and, nine years later, Miandad was unlikely to be intimidated by anything Hughes would throw in his direction. In fact, the batsman launched the first verbal assault by describing Hughes as **'a fat bus conductor'** during an exchange between the pair.

Clearly fired up, the Australian had Miandad caught by Peter Taylor

MY FAVOURITE SLEDGE

When two sledgers collide: Dennis Lillee and Javed Miandad leave the umpire in an exposed position...

soon after and, as Hughes wheeled away in delight to celebrate with his team-mates, he jogged past the departing Pakistan number five and yelled:
'Tickets please!'

'It's all about the response,' said the British Hughes. 'The quick response to the comment from the batsman showed his clever wit. He was a bit of a wag really, and he'd always give a good retort.'

CHAPTER EIGHT

THE UMPIRES STRIKE BACK

Most people think they just stand around with any number of jumpers and hats hanging off them, but sometimes umpires like to join the sledging party too. **The only men on the pitch with genuine authority,** despite what captains and fast bowlers may think, the officials just can't help themselves, as this selection of incidents proves. Although, occasionally, they can come under fire themselves...

▓ THE UMPIRE'S DECISION IS NOT FINAL

It's possible that W.G. Grace's immense stature in the game back in the day led many umpires to cower away from making decisions that went against him. And with almost 55,000 runs to his name by the time he finally called time on his career, who were they to give him out? One famous example occurred in an exhibition match in which Grace was the main attraction for the gathered masses.

Grace vowed never to shave again until he was finally given out.

Not long into his innings – or certainly not long enough for him – Grace was clean bowled. Without saying a word, 'The Doctor' picked up the bails and placed them back on top of his stumps. He turned around to face the disbelieving bowler and said: 'They've come here to see me bat, not to see you bowl.'

Incredibly, the umpire did not bat an eyelid and Grace continued his innings to the delight of the large crowd.

▦ BAILED OUT

But not every umpire fell for the allure of the batting maestro. Grace was up to his old tricks again in another game, as he replaced a bail back on to the stumps after being bowled. This time, he pleaded with the umpire: ''Twas the wind which took the bail off.'

The umpire was having none of it and replied: 'Indeed, Doctor. And let us hope the wind helps the good doctor on thy journey back to the pavilion.'

▦ LONG OFF

The Lancashire League has never had a shortage of characters playing, but that also applied to the officials, notably George Long. During one match, the burly Australian Cecil 'Cec' Pepper, an entertaining individual himself who made a full-time job out of haranguing the officials, was bowling and launched a vociferous appeal for leg before.

Long was unmoved and Pepper, in his uniquely explosive style, unleashed a foul-mouthed tirade in frustration at not being given the decision. At the end of the over, Long was approached by a remorseful Pepper, who sought forgiveness for his behaviour by way of a grovelling apology.

'Don't worry, Cec,' said Long. 'Up here we like a man that speaks his mind.'

Encouraged by Long's camaraderie, Pepper once again launched a ferocious appeal for lbw in his following over. As he looked hopefully towards the umpire with his arms raised, Long shook his head and said: 'Not out, you fat Australian bastard!'

▓ FEISTY BIRD

The Australian sledging star Merv Hughes was always keen for a bit of gentle banter with the umpires, and he had an amusing exchange with legendary English official Dickie Bird during an Ashes Test in England.

As Hughes returned to his mark following a dot ball, he asked Bird how far into the over he was: 'Is that three I've had or is that three to come?'

Bird wasted no time with his no-nonsense reply: 'Shut up, Merv or I'll no-ball you for being a smart arse!'

▓ ONE NEL TO THE UMPIRE

Australian umpire Simon Taufel has established himself as one of the international game's premier officials – and he has an interesting take on sledging. During a Pakistan v South Africa Test series that was played on the sub-continent, visiting bowler Andre Nel was performing his trademark routine against home batsman Shoaib Malik.

Nel, as already discussed, is certainly not a shy cricketer, and following a lengthy and repeated spate of verbal maulings to Malik, Taufel stepped in and asked Nel's captain to join him and the bowler.

Expecting the worst, skipper Graeme Smith approached Nel and Taufel, only for the umpire to inform him: 'Look, he's only traipsing out one line; it's getting a bit boring.' For once, Nel was silenced.

▓ MAKING PLANS

If the banter between players heats up a little too much for the liking of an umpire, they're obliged to step in to defuse the situation. Of course, by taking such action, an official leaves himself open to becoming part of the fun. This was very much the case when Warwickshire were playing Northamptonshire in a crucial top-of-the-table County Championship clash in 1995 and Allan Donald was laying into Russell Warren.

The South African was still miffed that Warren had been dropped when he'd yet to get off the mark and, by the time he'd reached 70, Donald had had enough and let rip with a torrent of Afrikaans abuse.

Umpire Ken Palmer had also had enough and intervened: 'Come on, Springbok. Let's just get on with it.'

'It's OK,' replied Donald. 'I'm just asking him where he's going for a drink tonight.'

BLUE PETER

One of the most extraordinary cases of umpire sledging occurred during the Boxing Day Ashes Test at Melbourne in 1990. England, on their way to a second successive defeat in the series, had handed a debut to spinner Phil Tufnell, who had already made an impression on the tour by being fined for returning to the team hotel from a night out at 8.30 am.

Sydney, 1991, and Phil Tufnell is struggling after another heavy night...

During Australia's successful run chase on the final day, a wicketless Tufnell was bowling and asked Aussie umpire Peter McConnell how many balls were left in the over. 'Count 'em yourself, you Pommie bastard!' was McConnell's sensationally rude response.

'Sorry? You what?' replied an incredulous Tufnell. 'Look mate, all I did was ask you how many balls there were to go in the over.'

Even Tufnell's captain Graham Gooch became involved in the incident, telling the umpire he could not talk to his players like that. Soon after, Tufnell thought David Boon had edged one into wicketkeeper Jack Russell's gloves and he was celebrating his first Test wicket, until McConnell said loud and clear: 'Not out.'

Apoplectic with rage, Tufnell volleyed back: 'You fucking bastard!'

'Now,' replied McConnell. '*You* can't talk to *me* like that!'

▦ CRAFTY COCKNEY

As a direct consequence of that incident, another Aussie umpire was the victim of a Tufnell sledge in the next Test at Sydney. In a match where McConnell was once again playing hard to get in terms of giving batsmen out, his fellow official was Tony Crafter, and Tufnell was bowling from his end.

After much toil, the spinner finally picked up his first Test wicket when Greg Matthews holed out for 128 to Eddie Hemmings at mid-off. In mid-celebration, Tufnell screamed at innocent party Crafter: 'I suppose that's not fucking out either!'

BOOZEHOUND BILL

Without a doubt the most unusual and equally hilarious example of unorthodox umpiring came in 1936 when Middlesex were playing Sussex. Bill Bestwick gave a young Denis Compton, batting at number eleven, out leg before with a decision that seemed dubious to say the least.

The umpire, a renowned boozer who was forced to have a chaperone with him during his playing career so he wouldn't slip off for a drink, then had to face the wrath of Middlesex and England captain Gubby Allen. Amazingly, Bestwick admitted to Allen that he had given the 18-year-old Compton out because he was desperate for the toilet and would have wet himself had the innings not ended there and then.

BIRDSONG

English umpire John Hampshire, confusingly a former Derbyshire, Leicestershire and Yorkshire player, was never afraid to tell it like it was – probably because he was born in Yorkshire.

During an early-season county match involving Essex, Ronnie Irani was getting firmly stuck into an opposition batsman when Hampshire decided to step in. As Irani recalled: 'Hampshire said: "Have you been on birdseed all winter or what?"

'So I said: "What do you mean, John?"

'He replied: "All you're doing is chirping every two minutes – concentrate on your game, lad!"

'It was a good comeback and it shut me up.'

BLIND ALLEY

Bill Alley was another of the legendary 'old school' umpires who moved over to England from Australia to play cricket. After a successful career as an all-rounder, Alley began officiating and his attitude was slightly more relaxed than the likes of Billy Bowden or Alim Dar's.

During a county match, Alley noticed that Lancashire bowler Peter Lee appeared to be tampering with the ball. The umpire, who was probably not entirely innocent of seam-fiddling himself during his playing career, asked to inspect the ball. Upon closer examination, Alley realised his suspicions were confirmed and he turned to Lee and said: 'You've done a great job with that. If you don't get seven wickets with it, I'll report you!'

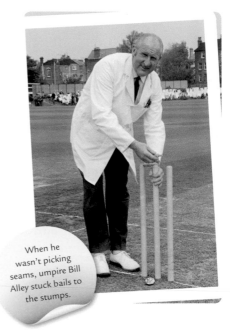

When he wasn't picking seams, umpire Bill Alley stuck bails to the stumps.

NIGHT VISION

The 1971 Gillette Cup semi-final between Lancashire and Gloucestershire will never be forgotten by anyone who was at Old Trafford. Late one summer's evening, 27,000 people were kept on the edge of their seats by an enthralling match that had been delayed by about an hour's rain at lunchtime.

As a consequence, the home team won the game in virtual darkness after umpires Arthur Jepson and Dickie Bird decided to play to a finish that evening. But, as the darkness was descending, an exchange that was as memorable as the match took place between Lancashire captain Jack Bond, who eventually hit the winning run, and Jepson.

Bond was unhappy about batting in the poor light and made his point to Jepson, who pointed to the sky and said: 'What's that?'

'The moon,' replied a puzzled Bond.

'Well, how bloody far do you want to see?' said Jepson.

FASTEST FINGER

The umpire is always right, of course, except when he is wrong, but that doesn't help if he readily admits he is wrong long after giving someone out. Mike Brearley was on the receiving end of such a calamity, which qualifies as a sledge as it added a fair deal of insult to injury.

During the fourth Test of England's 1976-77 tour of India, Brearley edged Bhagwath Chandrasekhar to Gundappa Viswanath and was given out for just four. The problem was that the ball had bounced before arriving in Viswanath's hands, yet umpire M.V. Nagendra still gave the decision.

An unusually distraught Brearley was eating his lunch in the pavilion when Mr Nagendra paid him a visit to apologise for the duff decision. 'Mr Brearley, I am very sorry,' said the umpire. 'I knew it was not out, but I felt my finger going up and I just couldn't stop it.'

Well, that's all right then.

UMPIRING BY NUMBERS

Windies quickie Michel Holding was once bowling in Australia and was convinced he'd trapped an opponent leg before. As he watched the ball cannon straight into the Aussie batsman's pads, he launched a vociferous and passionate appeal, only to draw a blank from the umpire, who declared 'not out'.

Holding continued to bowl and the umpire duly said 'over' when the West Indian had completed his allotted deliveries. As Holding retrieved his hat from the official, he looked him in the eye and said: 'At least you can count to six.'

FAISALABAD FURY

No section on umpires, banter and sledging could possibly be complete without reference to the infamous spat between England captain Mike Gatting and Pakistani umpire Shakoor Rana at Faisalabad in 1987.

After a controversial first Test, in which England felt many decisions went against them, tensions were high as the tourists had Pakistan 106 for five at the end of day two, trailing by almost 200. Just before off-spinner Eddie Hemmings ran in to bowl, Gatting informed batsman Salim Malik that he was moving long leg David Capel closer in and, as the bowler started his run-up, the England captain signalled with his hand to Capel that he'd come close enough.

The moment the ball left Hemmings' hand, Rana galloped in from his square leg position, shouting at Gatting: 'Stop! Stop! You're waving your hand. That's cheating.'

He had interpreted the skipper's move as illegal, because he thought Gatting was making the fielding change as the ball was being bowled – unfortunately for him and Gatting, he was wrong and a brutal storm blew up there and then.

Television pictures of Gatting and Rana going nose-to-nose, furiously yelling and finger-jabbing at each other were relayed all over the world and a major diplomatic incident was underway – even the British Foreign Office were involved. Most of what was said will always remain between Gatting and Rana, but what is known is that Rana called Gatting 'a fucking cheat' and informed him that his actions were against the rules.

To this, Gatting is believed to have responded: 'We made the rules.'

Pakistan Cricket Board president General Safdar Butt said at the time: 'Mike Gatting used some filthy language to the umpire, and let

Shakoor Rana warns Mike Gatting to keep quiet, or else he'll make sure the England captain is barred from every restaurant in Faisalabad.

me tell you, some of the less filthy words are "bastard" and "son of a bitch" and so on.'

As a result of the incident, there was no play on the third day, as Rana insisted Gatting had to apologise – which he eventually did – and England didn't tour Pakistan again for 13 years. Now that's *proper* controversy.

RONNIE IRANI

Former England all-rounder and talkSPORT presenter Ronnie Irani was never a player to shirk a challenge. So when his team-mates decided he was the man to capture the prize wicket of Sachin Tendulkar in a one-day international at Lord's, he didn't have a choice. Irani takes up the story:

'Tendulkar was the number one batsman in the world at the time and we were in the dressing room trying to figure out a way to get him out. Goughie said to me: "Ronnie, you're the one who's going to get Tendulkar out. He struggles with your type of bowling."

'I said: "What do you mean by that?"

"I'm a top bowler; I'm a great bowler," Gough replied. "Tendulkar loves great bowlers, he always plays well against great bowlers like me, Freddie [Flintoff] and Gilo [Ashley Giles]. You're the man for Tendulkar."

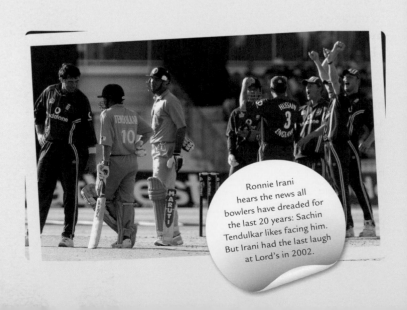

Ronnie Irani hears the news all bowlers have dreaded for the last 20 years: Sachin Tendulkar likes facing him. But Irani had the last laugh at Lord's in 2002.

'As it happens, Tendulkar had struggled slightly against me that series – I don't mean I'd tied him in knots, but the difference between him and Hayden, Gilchrist or Lara is that when you put it on a good line or length, Tendulkar respects it. He blocks it. If you're slightly off line or slightly off length, it goes for four or six – whichever he chooses. He does not hit a fielder. The other guys will take on a good ball, so you've always got a chance with those boys.

'Anyway, Tendulkar was on his way out to the middle, and I was thinking "How shall I get into him? Should I have a word with him, maybe?" I'm not a big fan of aggressive sledging or being nasty. I like to have a word with people, make them laugh or smile and then hopefully their concentration will go.

'So, when I was bowling and he was at the umpire's end, I said to him: **"Sachin, you've struggled with my bowling this series. You've been blocking me the whole time. What's all that about?"**

'To my amazement, he reacted. He turned to me and said: **"Ronnie, this is my three hundred and fifth one-day international. I like your bowling."**

'What do you say to that? There's no comeback to that, is there? I walked past him and as I went past Graham Thorpe at mid-on, I said: **"Hey, Thorpey! Did you hear that? What do you think?"**

"Tell Nasser to get you off quick!" he said.

'A couple of balls later, Tendulkar was on strike. I ran in from the Pavilion End, down the slope and I let this thing go at him. It just nipped back and hit him right on

MY FAVOURITE SLEDGE

the knee-roll. Now, I don't care where that thing's going. If I hit Tendulkar on the pads, it's got to be out! There was a massive appeal. Alec Stewart's gone up behind the stumps. Paul Collingwood is up at backward point and even Thorpey's gone up from mid-on.

'The umpire's finger went up – he's given him out. Sachin Tendulkar lbw bowled Irani at Lord's. We've gone berserk, absolutely mad.

'As it happened, Tendulkar went for a leg bye while I was appealing, and because he kept his eye on the ball, he actually ran into me, knocked me over and I fell on my backside. So as I got up, I said: **"Hey, Sachin. This is my fifth one-day international and I like your batting!"**'

CHAPTER NINE

STEAMING IN:

WHEN CRICKET CROWDS SLEDGE

What would a pantomime be without the audience participation? 'He's behind you!' and 'Oh no it isn't!' are as integral to any show as the cast and crew. Similarly, imagine a cricket match in which the crowd did not participate whatsoever. No polite applause, no cheers and no abusing the players fielding near them. **Yes, sledging can be just as entertaining between the crowd and the fielders as it can be between two players. In fact, some of the funniest moments in the game's recent history have come from the stands, so here we salute ourselves, the paying punters.**

▦ NOT A TALL STORY

Yorkshire's Scarborough festival is as raucous a cricket extravaganza as any up-for-it fan could hope to find. Paul Nixon was once playing for Kent in a limited-overs game on a Sunday in the Yorkshire seaside resort and there was a good atmosphere: 'The most partisan crowd is Sunday afternoon at Scarborough,' he said. 'It's always fun, from a dozen streakers to people dressed up.'

His Kent team were not enjoying a particularly good day, as the home side had made the most of the festival spirit being shown by the visitors' bowling. 'We'd gone all around the ground, so they put Matt Walker on to bowl,' explained the wicketkeeper.

'Walker is about five foot two tall and five foot two sideways. He's just about to set off and this bloke stands up in the crowd and bellows: "Hi-Hoooooo!" and the whole ground was crying with laughter. The comedy timing was brilliant.'

▦ A TALL STORY

Giraffe-like paceman Bob Willis was thrown straight in at the deep end when he made his Ashes Test debut at the age of 21 in front of a baying crowd in Sydney. Willis, who would go on to suffer the embarrassment of walking to the crease after a tea interval without his bat at Edgbaston, stood 6ft 6in tall and stuck out like a sore thumb patrolling the vast outfield of the SCG. And it wasn't long before he endured some debut humiliation when the locals got stuck right into him.

The Hill was a grassy area of the Sydney arena that used to be unseated and it has long been famous for its boisterous fans – as Willis was quick to discover. 'Hey, Willis!' yelled one fan. 'I didn't know they stacked shit that high!' while another screamed: 'You take ugly pills? You must be hooked on them!'

But Willis and his England team had the last laugh on that particular occasion, as he took a maiden Test wicket in a whopping 299-run victory for the tourists.

YABBA OF THE HILL

The most famous occupant of The Hill was, without doubt, one Stephen Harold Gascoigne, better known as 'Yabba'. He was an ordinary spectator, but no ordinary heckler, who would sit and cast judgement upon any cricket taking place at the SCG.

Among his sledging repartee was to shout to any wayward bowler 'Your length's lousy, but you bowl a good width!' or to anybody with whom he grew irate 'I wish you were a statue and I was a pigeon!' Once, when a batsman was adjusting his box, Yabba wisecracked: 'Those are the only balls you've touched all day!'

But perhaps Yabba's finest moment came during the Bodyline tour when Douglas Jardine was batting and became so irritated by a fly that kept heading his way that he attempted to swat it away with his bat. As Jardine wafted his bat around, Yabba yelled: 'Leave our flies alone. They're the only friends you've got!'

Today, anybody sitting in the area that used to be The Hill will find a bronze statue of a man with a tilted hat on his head and hand poised to the side of his mouth with his jaws wide open, leaning forward, ready to share his thoughts with the world. *That* is Yabba.

Yabba of The Hill – even the Aussie statues don't keep quiet at the SCG.

::: SALIM'LL FIX IT

Staying in Sydney, the fans there are rarely slow to catch on to a player's controversial past, and so it proved when Pakistan toured in 1995. The tourists' number five, Salim Malik, had been the subject of match-fixing allegations the previous year, when Australian stars Shane Warne, Mark Waugh and Tim May alleged that he'd offered them £130,000 each to lose a Test during a tour of Pakistan.

Malik strenuously denied the allegations, but that meant nothing to one wag in the stands. After the Pakistani was out in the first innings (lbw to McGrath) for 36, not a particularly bad score, he was walking back to the pavilion when someone shouted: 'The cheque's in the mail!'

Malik was eventually banned from cricket for life in 2000, although he was subsequently cleared of any wrongdoing by a Pakistan court in 2008.

::: WARM-UP MAN

If you can't beat them, join them. That's certainly what Ronnie Irani was thinking when thousands of Australians ganged up on him during a 2002 one-dayer in Sydney. The England and Essex all-rounder was already having a bad day, after being dismissed for a third-ball duck by Shane Warne. Then, as Australia were romping to victory in front of a packed crowd who'd certainly had their fill of alcohol, as it was a day/night fixture, captain Nasser Hussain asked Irani to loosen up as he wanted him to bowl.

As Irani began doing his stretches, he could hear huge cheers behind him, but it was only when he turned around to face the crowd that he could see thousands of Australians were mimicking his every warm-up move. And he can still see them like it was yesterday:

'I wasn't to know, but I turned around and there were about twelve thousand Australians copying me in two or three tiers of the Sydney Cricket Ground. It was really strange – a big roar every time I stretched my side muscles – Hooray! Hooray! So I joined in and had a bit of fun with the Aussies. When you go to Australia, you get pelters from the stand and there's only one way to react and that's positive and winning them over. You've got to be jolly with it.'

Two days later, the teams met again in Melbourne and, much to his amusement, the locals repeated the trick as Irani was preparing to bowl. A new craze had begun and, even today, clips of the incident have been viewed more than a million times on YouTube.

Ronnie Irani auditions for aerobics Oz-style.

 ## HOT UNDER THE COLLAR

Irani didn't find the Australian crowd so funny when he returned to Melbourne a year later for another one-day series. After toiling in the field for three and a half hours on a boiling hot Australian day, Irani was not necessarily in the mood for fun and games. Not only had Hussain bowled him straight through his ten overs without a break in the searing heat, but Irani also had to contend with a non-stop barrage of abuse from a spectator in the members' enclosure – an area where fans are required to dress appropriately and certainly not indulge in the kind of behaviour associated with The Hill at Sydney.

As the England players left the field for the change of innings, Irani decided to pay his chief tormentor (the spectator, not Hussain) a little visit: 'My brain wasn't engaged. I was so hot and I just thought "Right, I'll have you." In Australia, if a spectator goes on the pitch, it's an immediate five thousand dollar fine, so I went over to this guy and said "Hey, you! You've been an absolute disgrace, an absolute disgrace!"

'He said "You what?"'

'So I said: "I've said nothing to you, you've been on at me for three and a half hours, swearing at me and this is a members' bit here!"'

'Anyway, it turned out I was talking to the wrong guy! But the guy who had been doing it suddenly came flying down the steps, Cantona-style, and gave me another massive bullet of four-letter words and abuse. I thought "Great, I've got him here."

'I said to him: "If you've got a problem, mate, come out on the pitch and we'll sort it out." But he wouldn't succumb to it, so I got my drink bottle, took the top off and I just drenched him in Gatorade – all over his shirt and tie – I covered him. He needed cooling down! Luckily, I got away with it, although one of the newspapers did pick it up.'

▦ MEGAPHONE MADNESS

Pakistan captain Inzamam-ul-Haq went a step further than Irani during a limited-overs match against India that was played in Toronto, Canada. The teams were playing in North America in 1997 to take advantage of the area's huge expat communities. With no love lost between the two Asian nations, the fans certainly took no prisoners either, and one spectator succeeded in winding up the Pakistani to the point of no return.

Inzamam would already have been irate at his team's paltry total of 116 as India set about strolling to victory, but he was further incensed by a group of Indian fans when he went to field near the boundary.

Among those fans was a gentleman who, assisted by a megaphone, hurled abuse at the chubby Pakistani including 'Stand straight, fatso!' and 'Fat potato, rotten potato!'

At that point, Inzamam waded into the crowd to confront the man and, although it's unclear where the story came from, tried to attack him with a bat as all hell let loose. Eventually, the Pakistani had to be held back by security officials, as he repeatedly attempted to return to the stands and the game was delayed for close to an hour.

Only in (North) America...

FLICK OF THE WRIST

Just to up the ante even further, Pakistan's Shahid Afridi did manage to make contact with a spectator with his bat several years later. After watching South Africa pile up 392 runs in a limited-overs game at Centurion in 2007, Afridi would have been disappointed to be dismissed for just 17 to leave his country on 56 for three and pretty much out of the game.

As he climbed the steps to the dressing room, with fans on either side of him, he lashed out at one spectator who had stood up and harangued him. It was only a flick of the bat, but it was certainly unprofessional and, as a result, Afridi was banned for four matches, including the first two games of the World Cup.

TALES FROM THE FRONT LINE

On a lighter, less violent level, the Ashes has always been played with an intensity on the pitch, but since 1994, the crowd have more than played their part, too, thanks to the advent of the Barmy Army.

England's travelling cricket fans make a lot of noise wherever they are, which usually becomes louder as the day goes on and the drink goes in. Win, lose or draw, their sole ethos is about having fun – and winding up opposition players wherever possible. Just as in football, where the best players are always targeted for ridicule by opposition supporters, so it is with cricket.

Naturally, Shane Warne has come in for a great deal of stick from the Barmy Army – when he toured England in 1997, he was greeted at most grounds with the following football chant to the tune of 'Knees-up Mother Brown':

'Who ate all the pies?
Who ate all the pies?
You fat bastard!
You fat bastard!
You ate all the pies!'

The Barmy Army had an unusually liberal policy for new recruits – anyone will do.

On another tour of England eight years later, Warne had recently split from his wife, but the Barmy Army showed no mercy by repeatedly serenading him with the following line, to the tune of 'Chirpy Chirpy Cheep Cheep':

'Where's your missus gone?
Where's your missus gone?'

Later that summer, as England finally ended their long barren run by reclaiming the Ashes, courtesy of a nailbiting draw at The Oval, a chant of 'You're only good at swimming!' was heard coming from the Army, a reference to the fact that the Aussies had claimed 15 medals in the pool in the previous summer's Olympics.

⠿ LANGER LOSES IT

Despite their football-style chants and revelry, the Barmy Army never managed to offend any cricketers – until Justin Langer decided to take them on. During the 2002-03 Ashes tour to Australia, there had been reports that Brett Lee's bowling action may be investigated. Jumping on this bandwagon, every time Lee bowled throughout the series, the Barmy Army would scream, in unison, 'no ball!'

By the time of the Boxing Day Test at Melbourne, Langer had had enough and launched a vicious outburst against the English supporters: 'I thought they were a disgrace,' he said. 'These people are standing behind the fence, drinking beer, and most of them are about fifty kilograms overweight, making ridiculous comments. They pay their money and that sort of stuff, but there's still some integrity in life, I think.'

He was also rumoured to have exchanged words with several Army members in the following Test at Sydney, during a rare defeat, but the English fans were to have the last laugh, composing this song about their Australian foe to the tune of 'My Old Man's a Dustman':

'Langer is an Aussie
He wears the gold and green
He is the biggest whinger
That we have ever seen
He wasn't very happy
When we called Brett Lee's no ball
He's got a very big mouth
And he's only five feet tall.'

He who laughs last and all that...

■ BROAD SHOULDERS

Inevitably, the Australian fans realised they could also join in with sledging the English players (not that they hadn't before) in a more organised way and The Fanatics were born, although their support lent itself to all sports.

The Fanatics were out in full force at the 2009 Ashes in England and immediately set about taunting the home team's young all-rounder Stuart Broad, whose longish blond hair was a source of amusement. Whenever Broad found himself fielding near the stands, he was treated to a rendition of Aerosmith's 'Dude Looks Like A Lady' by The Fanatics. It's no coincidence that, these days, Broad cuts his hair much shorter.

The youngster was no stranger to crowd abuse after touring New Zealand the previous year. In a one-day game at Wellington, thousands of students had been given free tickets as part of their Freshers' Week packs, meaning the ground was full of drunk youngsters.

Broad was sent to field on the boundary and made the terrible mistake of allowing the ball to sneak through his legs and over the ropes for four – and the crowd didn't let him forget it either: 'I reckon that twenty thousand people were calling me that swearword you often hear from football crowds when they're talking to the referee,' explained Broad.

He meant they were calling him a wanker.

UNIM-PRESSED

Not everyone can keep up with the wild enthusiasm of cricket fans like the Barmy Army. For some spectators, the pace of the game can lead to drastic measures being taken. In the 1986-87 Ashes series, England led 1-0 going into the third Test at Adelaide and were quite content when the final day's play offered precious little in terms of entertainment as it petered out into a bore draw.

But nobody present at the South Australia ground could possibly have expected the lengths one female spectator would go to in an effort to keep herself occupied during the dull spectacle out in the middle. As the *Wisden Book of Test Cricket* noted: 'A female spectator set up an ironing board and attended to her laundry throughout the fifth day's play.'

Why didn't she just stay at home?

LAMB À L'ORANGE

An equally bizarre incident occurred during an England tour of India in the 1980s, again during a lifeless match that was heading for a draw. This time, poor weather had played its part in forcing the stalemate and the crowd were demanding some kind of entertainment – fortunately, England's Allan Lamb was on hand to provide it.

The South African-born batsman found a discarded orange in the field and, for reasons best known to him, hurled it towards the boundary, but managed to hit a policeman's helmet. Within minutes, hundreds of oranges appeared on the pitch next to where Lamb was fielding. These weren't thrown in anger towards him. They were merely further missiles for Lamb to use against the policeman...

▥ BLAST-A-CHEF

Staying with food, you have to give credit to some fans for doing their homework before launching a vocal attack on a player. During the 2005 Ashes tour, Australia were playing an English county side in a warm-up fixture when Matthew Hayden was out early on without causing the scorers much difficulty.

The opening batsman had recently written his own cookery book, and someone in the crowd was either privy to this information or had possibly even sampled the tome. So, as Hayden trotted back to the changing room, one of the most bizarre sledges was heard echoing around the ground: 'Hayden, you're shit and so is your chicken casserole!'

Another Aussie working the barbie: cook book author Matthew Hayden seemingly viewing grilled chicken for the first time in his life.

▥ BOARD STIFF

With so many county matches in England played on weekdays, when most people tend to be at work, there are often very few people in the stands. This can lead to hilarious moments, as spectators' conversations can often be heard echoing around the empty ground.

Once, in Northampton, Lancashire bowler Peter Lee was the unfortunate recipient of crowd abuse from such a situation when two hard-of-hearing fans had a rather loud discussion. As Lee prepared to return to the attack, one gentlemen said: 'Oh no, they're putting Boards on.'

The other fellow replied: 'Who's Boards?'

'This bloke coming on. Boards. Every time they put him on they keep hitting it to the boards.'

David Lloyd, who was playing in that match, reflected: 'You're far worse off as a player in that situation than with ninety thousand watching at the MCG.'

THE 11TH COMMANDMENT

A more concerted effort at sledging came from a West Indian spectator during the 1973 Test series against Australia. For the first Test at Sabina Park, the Windies had recalled paceman Uton Dowe, who had played only three times previously, but he suffered something of a mauling at the hands of Australian opener Keith Stackpole and was soon replaced.

It was not until much later in the day that captain Rohan Kanhai decided to give Dowe another chance but, as he made the change and the bowler began to mark out his run, a fan yelled: 'Hey Kanhai, you forgotten the eleventh commandment? Dowe shalt not bowl!'

FIRED UP

A less subtle crowd reaction also occurred in the Caribbean. Instances of cricket crowd trouble are few and far between – but one unfortunate incident led to a reprieve for Viv Richards.

With a wave of hype behind him, Richards was making his debut for Antigua against St Kitts, but was given out early on, adjudged to have been caught behind. The batsman was certain he hadn't made contact, and did not hide his feelings as he walked back to the dressing room.

That display of aggression and injustice ignited the crowd, who had soon set fire to one of the stands. Fearing they had little choice, the league administrators offered Richards another chance to bat, and the Antiguan was grateful for the opportunity. Sadly for him, and the crowd, he made another duck.

▦ GIVING THE BIRD

Cambridge University bowler John Warr was called up for the disastrous Ashes tour of 1950-51, when a poor team were thrashed 4-1 by the Aussies. One particular Australian didn't even have the courtesy to wait for Warr to take the field before heckling him.

As Warr set foot on Australian soil, a labourer bellowed: 'You have as much chance of taking a Test wicket on this tour as I have of pushing a pound of butter up a parrot's arse with a hot needle.'

But the Aussie was wrong. Warr did take a wicket. Literally. Just one. And nobody ever found out what happened to the parrot.

▦ TUFF AT THE TOP

It's traditional to leave the best until last, and so to a classic moment from another Ashes series, this time the 1994-95 contest Down Under. The Australian crowds love nothing more than a duel with an England fielder. All tourists have been targeted at one point, with Alan Mullally once having to endure questions like 'Are you going for the Audi rings or the Olympic rings?' due to his prolific tally of consecutive ducks.

There's no sympathy from team-mates either, as Darren Gough revealed: 'You do chuckle to yourself on the pitch when you hear these things.'

And there was a great deal of chuckling when a fan confronted Phil Tufnell. The Middlesex bowler was another Aussie crowd favourite. He'd already made a name for himself for all the wrong reasons when he had first toured in 1990-91. Thanks to a combination of his hapless fielding and woeful batting, the more-than-respectable left-arm spinner was singled out for a barrage of insults and abuse from the stands wherever he went.

After one particularly poor misfield, 'Tuffers', as he had become affectionately known, was on the receiving end once again and, when the noise died down, one loud comment rang around the ground and induced laughter from other fans and even the players: 'Oy, Tuffers! Can I borrow your brain? I'm building an idiot.'

Phil Tufnell tries to box with a kangaroo, but was soon knocked out in the first round.

▦ THE talkSPORT TOP 10 SLEDGES

10

ADAM PARORE v MARK WAUGH

Mark Waugh welcomes Adam Parore to the wicket: 'Oh, I remember you from a couple of years ago in Australia. You were shit then and you're fucking useless now.'

Parore replies: 'Yeah, that's me, and when I was there you were going out with that old ugly slut. Now I hear you've married her, you dumb c***.'

9

GLENN MCGRATH v RAMNARESH SARWAN

Glenn McGrath cannot dismiss Ramnaresh Sarwan and asks him: 'So what does Brian Lara's cock taste like?'

The youngster immediately replies: 'I don't know. Ask your wife.'

McGrath explodes and storms down the wicket to confront Sarwan: 'You mention my fucking wife again and I'll rip your fucking throat out!'

8

IAN HEALY v MIKE ATHERTON

Ian Healy confronts Mike Atherton in Sydney when the Englishman stands his ground after apparently edging and being caught behind: 'You're a fucking cheat!'

Atherton quietly responds: 'When in Rome, dear boy…'

7

IAN BOTHAM v ROD MARSH

Rod Marsh greets Ian Botham's arrival at the crease: 'So how's your wife and my kids?'

Botham instantly answers: 'The wife's fine, but the kids are retarded.'

6

MERV HUGHES v ROBIN SMITH

Robin Smith plays and misses a ball from Merv Hughes, who says: 'You can't fucking bat!'

Smith then hits the next Hughes ball for four and replies: 'Hey Merv! We make a fine pair. I can't fucking bat and you can't fucking bowl!'

5

DARYLL CULLINAN v SHANE WARNE

Chubby Shane Warne welcomes his South African 'rabbit' Daryll Cullinan to the crease: 'I've been waiting two years for another chance to humiliate you.'

Cullinan replies: 'Looks like you spent it eating.'

4

MARK WAUGH v JAMES ORMOND

Mark Waugh, brother of Australia captain Steve, makes fun of England's James Ormond: 'What the fuck are you doing out here? Surely you're not good enough to play for England?'

'Maybe not,' replies Ormond, 'But at least I'm the best player in my family.'

3

VIV RICHARDS v GREG THOMAS

Greg Thomas sarcastically tells the playing-and-missing Viv Richards: 'It's red, round and weighs about five ounces, in case you were wondering.'

Richards hits the next ball out of the ground and calmly replies: 'You know what it looks like, now you go and find it.'

2

MERV HUGHES v JAVED MIANDAD

Javed Miandad calls Merv Hughes 'a fat bus conductor' during a heated exchange between the pair. Hughes has Miandad caught soon after and runs past the Pakistani, yelling: 'Tickets please!'

1

GLENN MCGRATH v EDDO BRANDES

An angry Glenn McGrath can't get Eddo Brandes out so asks him: 'Why are you so fat?' The portly Zimbabwean retorts...

'Because every time
I make love to your wife,
she gives me a biscuit!'

Eddo Brandes,
the chicken farmer
whose biscuit-based
diet left Glenn McGrath
speechless.

BIBLIOGRAPHY

In the course of researching this book, the following resources were used:

Mad Dogs and the Englishman, David English (Virgin, 2002)

The Best of Enemies: Whingeing Poms Versus Arrogant Aussies, Patrick Kidd and Peter McGuinness (Know the Score, 2009)

Flying Stumps and Metal Bars: Cricket's Greatest Moments by the People Who Were There, Wisden Cricketer (Aurum Press, 2008)

The Wit of Cricket, Barry Johnston (Hodder & Stoughton, 2009)

The Spirit of Cricket, Rob Smyth (Elliott & Thompson Ltd, 2010)

What Now? The Autobiography, Phil Tufnell (Collins Willow, 1999)

Cricket Mad, Michael Parkinson (Stanley Paul, 1969)

smh.com.au
theage.com.au
dailytelegraph.com.au
cricinfo.com
independent.co.uk
guardian.co.uk
thetimes.co.uk
telegraph.co.uk
dailymail.co.uk
mirror.co.uk
thesun.co.uk
sport.co.uk
talksport.net/mag
redbulletin.co.uk
bbc.co.uk
skysports.com
telegraphindia.com